Modern-Day Pirates

by John M. Dunn

LUCENT BOOKS

A part of Gale, Cengage Learning

GALE
CENGAGE Learning™

Detroit • New York • San Francisco • New Haven, Conn • Waterville, Maine • London

GALE
CENGAGE Learning™

LIBRARY OF CONGRESS CATALOGING-IN-PUBLICATION DATA

Dunn, John M., 1949-
  Modern-day pirates / by John M. Dunn.
    p. cm. -- (Hot topics)
  Includes bibliographical references and index.
  ISBN 978-1-4205-0351-7 (hardcover)
  1. Pirates. 2. Piracy. 3. Hijacking of ships. I. Title.
  G535.D85 2012
  364.16'4--dc23

                                              2011020438

Lucent Books
27500 Drake Rd.
Farmington Hills, MI 48331

ISBN-13: 978-1-4205-0351-7
ISBN-10: 1-4205-0351-0

Printed in the United States of America
1 2 3 4 5 6 7 15 14 13 12 11

Printed by Bang Printing, Brainerd, MN, 1st Ptg., 08/2011

CONTENTS

FOREWORD

Young people today are bombarded with information. Aside from traditional sources such as newspapers, television, and the radio, they are inundated with a nearly continuous stream of data from electronic media. They send and receive e-mails and instant messages, read and write online "blogs," participate in chat rooms and forums, and surf the web for hours. This trend is likely to continue. As Patricia Senn Breivik, the former dean of university libraries at Wayne State University in Detroit, has stated, "Information overload will only increase in the future. By 2020, for example, the available body of information is expected to double every 73 days! How will these students find the information they need in this coming tidal wave of information?"

Ironically, this overabundance of information can actually impede efforts to understand complex issues. Whether the topic is abortion, the death penalty, gay rights, or obesity, the deluge of fact and opinion that floods the print and electronic media is overwhelming. The news media report the results of polls and studies that contradict one another. Cable news shows, talk radio programs, and newspaper editorials promote narrow viewpoints and omit facts that challenge their own political biases. The World Wide Web is an electronic minefield where legitimate scholars compete with the postings of ordinary citizens who may or may not be well-informed or capable of reasoned argument. At times, strongly worded testimonials and opinion pieces both in print and electronic media are presented as factual accounts.

Conflicting quotes and statistics can confuse even the most diligent researchers. A good example of this is the question of whether or not the death penalty deters crime. For instance, one study found that murders decreased by nearly one-third when the death penalty was reinstated in New York in 1995. Death penalty supporters cite this finding to support their argument that the existence of the death penalty deters criminals from committing murder. However, another study found that states without the death penalty have murder rates below the national average. This study is cited by opponents of capital punishment, who reject the claim that the death penalty deters murder. Students need context and clear, informed discussion if they are to think critically and make informed decisions.

The Hot Topics series is designed to help young people wade through the glut of fact, opinion, and rhetoric so that they can think critically about controversial issues. Only by reading and thinking critically will they be able to formulate a viewpoint that is not simply the parroted views of others. Each volume of the series focuses on one of today's most pressing social issues and provides a balanced overview of the topic. Carefully crafted narrative, fully documented primary and secondary source quotes, informative sidebars, and study questions all provide excellent starting points for research and discussion. Full-color photographs and charts enhance all volumes in the series. With its many useful features, the Hot Topics series is a valuable resource for young people struggling to understand the pressing issues of the modern era.

INTRODUCTION

ANARCHY AT SEA

In the early twenty-first century sea piracy is one of the world's hottest issues. The news media teem with daily reports of heavily armed pirates raiding huge cargo ships, luxury yachts, ocean oil rigs, and even small fishing boats around the globe. Pirates also hijack ships and take prisoners whom they hold for ransom. "At the end of 2010, around 500 seafarers from more than 18 countries are being held hostage by pirates,"[1] according to a study from the Colorado-based think tank, One Earth Future.

Such high-seas drama is not just the stuff of fascinating news stories. Maritime piracy also represents a real and growing danger to passengers and crews. It also threatens to disrupt maritime trade, which composes from 80 to 90 percent of all commercial traffic in the world and is valued at about $6 trillion.

In addition pirates now pose a threat to the world's energy supply. This danger became clear in 2009, when Somalian pirates in the Gulf of Aden hijacked a ship known as a very large crude carrier (VLCC) that was transporting 2 million barrels of oil. Since then there have been other attacks on oil tankers. In March 2011, for example, pirates using rocket-propelled guns and grenades hijacked the United Arab Emirates–flagged oil tanker *Zirku* on the East African coast.

Though piracy is making headlines today, the practice is nothing new. Rather, this brand of criminality is as old as sea travel itself. Stories of sea bandits date back at least two thousand years to the days of the Roman Empire. By the eighth century A.D. Viking sea warriors from Scandinavia (Denmark, Norway, and Sweden) were pillaging coastal settlements of Western Europe.

A thousand years later marauders attacked European merchant ships; meanwhile their Japanese counterparts, the Wokou pirates, terrorized ships in the Far East.

During the sixteenth and seventeenth centuries European monarchs hired their own pirates, called privateers, to attack rival nations in the waters of the New World. This government-sponsored wartime piracy paved the way for the so-called golden age of piracy, when legendary pirates such as Blackbeard and Captain Kidd menaced the islands of the Caribbean Sea. During the nineteenth century American ships had to fend off pirate attacks along the Barbary Coast—a term Europeans once used for the middle and western coastal regions of North Africa. Piracy in its many forms flourished until new, steam-powered ships helped militaries and law enforcement agencies of the world curtail it in the early twentieth century. After decades of relative calm on the seas, however, piracy has reemerged in recent years on a scale not seen before, thanks to a perfect storm of political, economic, and social forces.

Novels, motion pictures, and even theme parks often portray pirates as colorful, dashing, rascally adventurers with black eye patches, wielding swords and blunderbuss pistols, drinking rum and seeking treasure while sailing their wooden ships and flying their pirate flags adorned with the skull and crossbones.

Real piracy, however, is not, and never was, romantic. Pirates past and present are thugs and criminals. They are malicious, brutal, and often murderous. Their victims come from many walks of life. Some are poor people who, like many pirates themselves, are simple fishermen. Other victims include ship's officers and crew members, many of whom are from the poorer nations of the world. A few are rich passengers who travel on luxury yachts and are worth more to the pirates for ransom than their expensive vessels are. Even desperate refugees in dangerously overcrowded vessels who are fleeing oppression, war, or poverty in their homelands have been robbed, molested, and killed by callous and cruel pirates in modern times.

Today's pirates, unlike those of the past, use an array of highly developed deadly weapons, such as automatic rifles and hand

Pirates like Blackbeard ruled the Caribbean in the sixteenth and seventeenth centuries. The period was considered the golden age of piracy.

grenades, to carry out their maritime crimes. Many also rely on sophisticated navigational equipment and high-tech communications gear to stalk and zero in on their victims. Day and night, modern pirates strike vessels big and small along the coasts of China, Singapore, Africa, India, South America, Bangladesh, Indonesia, the Caribbean islands, and Africa, including Nigeria and Somalia, where 40 percent of all pirate attacks occur.

Piracy's impact is especially destructive in poor countries, where pirates, who are seldom pursued by law enforcement officials, are free to terrorize local populations. Making matters worse, many pirates also venture into other criminal activities, such as illicit trafficking in stolen goods, drugs, weapons, and human beings. Some join international crime syndicates. A few may be helping terrorist organizations to finance and carry out terrorist attacks.

Despite their recent gains, however, pirates themselves are now under attack. After years of relative inaction, scores of nations have made fighting pirates a top priority. Many have banded together and sent warships to escort commercial vessels through the most dangerous pirate zones. Nations are also negotiating treaties to modernize international piracy laws to enhance antipiracy measures and bring pirates to justice.

Successful antipiracy actions, however, are tough to carry out. For one thing, the world's oceans and seas are vast lawless regions that are hard to patrol. Confronting and capturing dangerous pirates is hard, dangerous, and expensive. Tricky legal problems often emerge when pirates are taken as prisoners. Who, for example, has the responsibility, or authority, to arrest and prosecute those accused of committing crimes on the open seas that lay beyond the legal jurisdiction of any country? Which nation pays for antipiracy enforcement? Are pirate suspects entitled to human rights protection no matter where they stand trial? What compensation is due piracy's victims? As the world community debates such issues and seeks answers, the issue of global piracy grows hotter every day.

THE RISE OF MODERN PIRATES

Pirates had a busy year in 2010. According to a study from the International Maritime Bureau's Piracy Reporting Centre (IMB PRC), a nonprofit investigative and information-sharing organization funded mainly by the shipping industry, "More people were taken hostage at sea in 2010 than in any year on record. . . . Pirates captured 1,181 seafarers and killed eight. A total of 53 ships were hijacked."[2] The study reveals that the number of pirate attacks has gone up annually during the last four years. The IMB also reports that there were 445 reported ship attacks in 2010—an increase of 10 percent from the year before. "These figures for the number of hostages and vessels taken are the highest we have ever seen," said Captain Pottengal Mukundan, director of the IMB PRC. "The continued increase in these numbers is alarming."[3]

Such numbers, however, most likely understate how serious the piracy problem is. Many experts think the real number of pirate attacks is considerably higher—maybe as much as 50 percent or more higher—because many, if not most, incidents are never reported. Rather than reporting piracy, many shipping companies discreetly pay ransoms demanded by pirates because it is often cheaper to pay the ransom than to lose cargo or miss a shipping deadline. Some firms also wish to conceal piracy problems from their insurance companies, fearing their insurance premiums will rise. They also do not want to encourage more piracy, by publicizing that their companies are willing to pay ransoms.

The Faces of Modern Piracy

Who are these modern pirates? In his book *Dangerous Waters: Modern Piracy and Terror on the High Seas,* author and seafarer John S. Burnett provides an answer:

> Many of today's pirates are organized groups of poverty-stricken young men living alongside busy shipping lanes who attack slow-moving ships that lumber by, rich pickings and perfect targets of opportunity. There are others who are far more brutal, ruthless, and cold blooded, who kill. They pack grenade launchers, anti-tank missiles, and assault rifles. . . . Many are employed by warlords, corrupt government officials, transnational crime organizations, and terrorist cells.[4]

A group of Somali pirates with rocket-propelled grenades prepares for a raid. Pirates use small, fast boats that come either from shore or from pirate mother ships at sea.

The Global Spread of Piracy

The IMB (International Maritime Bureau) warns mariners "to be extra cautious and to take necessary precautionary measures" against piracy in these areas (list is updated through May 2011).

Southeast Asia & India Sub-continent

- Bangladesh
- Indonesia
- Malacca Straits
- Malaysia
- Philippines
- Singapore Straits
- South China Sea
- Vietnam

South & Central America & the Caribbean Waters

- Brazil
- Haiti: Port au Prince
- Peru
- Venezuela

Africa and Red Sea

- Lagos and Bonny River (Nigeria)
- Conakry (Guinea)
- Douala Outer Anchorage (Cameroon)
- Gulf of Aden/Red Sea
- Somalia

Rest of the World

- Arabian Sea/Off Oman
- Indian Ocean/Off Seychelles/ Off Madagascar/Off West Maldives/Off Mozambique

Taken from: IMB.

Piracy and Armed Robbery 2005–2010

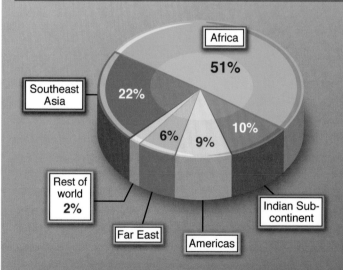

- Africa 51%
- Southeast Asia 22%
- Indian Sub-continent 10%
- Americas 9%
- Far East 6%
- Rest of world 2%

Taken from: Piracy Prone Areas and Warnings. ICC International Maritime Bureau (IMB). www.icc-ccs.org/piracy-reporting-centre/prone-areas-and-warnings.

Experts on piracy often classify modern pirates into three groups. The IMB's Pottengal Mukundan explains: "At the bottom end of the scale you have mugging at sea, where low-level criminals try to get on board a ship and try to steal whatever they can within a period of about forty minutes to an hour and then take off."[5] Many of these pirates are poor fishermen who prey on fellow fishermen in small boats usually not more than 50 miles (80.4km) offshore and rob them of their personal belongings and then leave. These seaborne muggers usually lack the experience, nerve, and resources to attempt boarding big, commercial vessels.

A NEW BREED OF PIRATES

"Modern-day pirates are not like Errol Flynn or Johnny Depp swinging through the rigging, but well-armed militiamen equipped with rocket-propelled grenades, assault rifles, global positioning systems and high-speed motorboats who have long terrorized the shipping lanes in the Gulf of Aden and literally gotten away with murder."—John S. Burnett, a former legislative assistant for members of Congress in Washington and author of *Dangerous Waters, Modern Piracy and Terror on the High Seas*

John S. Burnett. "Captain Kidd, Human-Rights Victim." *New York Times*, April 20, 2008. www.nytimes.com/2008/04/20/opinion/20burnett.html.

Second-level pirates, however, do have the background, skills, and assets to successfully hijack even the largest commercial ships in the world. Among their ranks are skilled individuals. Some are former soldiers. Others have specialized technical skills in electronics, high-tech communications, and navigational and tracking technology to monitor the movements of the targeted ships.

Unlike lower-level pirates, this mid-range group of sea bandits often makes use of a "mother ship," which is often a stolen fishing trawler or an even bigger craft. Somalian pirates, for example, seized a much larger vessel, the bulk cargo carrier MV *Sinar Kudus*, in the North Arabian Sea on March 16, 2011, and used it almost immediately as a mother ship to launch a raid on another ship. Regardless of its size, the mother ship carries its pirate crew far out to sea in search of cargo-bearing container ships or tankers that transport oil, coal, or chemicals.

Some pirates wait patiently on these mother ships, often pretending to be fishermen, until darkness comes. Then they shove off in smaller boats that they have kept on the mother ship. Some pirates try to sneak up to their targets in the darkness and board them. Ships with low running boards make this relatively easy to accomplish. If necessary, however, specially trained pirates use grappling hooks and ladders to get aboard. Somalian pirates are known to have hoisted themselves 300 feet (91.4m) up the side of a huge oil tanker, as it pitched and rolled in a rough sea, before they hijacked it.

Other pirate gangs prefer broad daylight to launch surprise attacks in small boats, firing their automatic weapons to intimidate a ship's crew. Often a few shots prove to be enough to capture a merchant ship. Once aboard the pirates try to commandeer the vessel and kidnap the captain, crew, and any passengers to be held as hostages.

Attacks like these are usually well planned. The pirates often know in advance exactly who their victims will be and how they plan to hijack their ships. Aiding them are spies in harbors and shipyards who provide information about various departing ships, their cargoes, and destinations. Sometimes a pirate gang sends out one of its own to work as a crew member aboard a targeted ship. Once the ship is under way, the spy tries to gather information about the voyage, which he secretly transmits to other fellow pirates who will carry out the upcoming attack.

Once the sea raiders have gained experience at this advanced level of piracy, many will enter the highest level of criminality in the world of pirating.

Crime Syndicates

Third-level pirates, the most sophisticated criminals of the sea, carry out the most lucrative and daring acts of modern piracy. Many belong to organized crime syndicates. Some pirate groups even take part in a process called "unionizing" that

Pirates in a speedboat approach one of their mother ships off the coast of Somalia.

brings together, or unifies, various crime syndicates into even larger criminal organizations. This process, according to law enforcement authorities, is well under way in Asian countries such as Hong Kong, mainland China, Singapore, Thailand, and Jakarta, where crime syndicates also traffic in human beings, weapons, and illicit drugs.

These third-level lords of piracy command ships and speedboats seaworthy enough to carry out attacks hundreds of miles out to sea. In areas that were once considered safe, crews aboard merchant ships now must be constantly on their guard.

Those who operate at this peak performance of piracy are often rich and powerful enough to proclaim themselves the prevailing power over large swaths of ocean and coastal areas, in a manner similar to drug cartels that control large areas in Central and South America. Now and then some pirate groups even try to exert influence over a nation's government. "They don't necessarily want to replace the government, but they want to have greater control so that their criminal enterprises can operate without interference," says Max Manwaring, professor of military strategy at the U.S. Army War College at Carlisle Barracks Garrison in Pennsylvania. "It's only when governments are in danger of having their power taken away, that the outside world begins to take piracy seriously."[6]

Pirate Dirty Work

Some of the world's most ruthless pirates are those that prey upon ships in Asian waters. Ransom is not always their biggest priority. Instead, they often force kidnapped crew members to steer the ship to a distant port where the pirates sell the stolen cargo to a corrupt buyer doing business on the black market, where illegal trade takes place. The pirates often paint over the

Garb of the Modern Caribbean Pirate

Guy Matthews, a Houston, Texas–based insurance adjustor and marine surveyor, writing for the Blue Water Insurance Company—an insurer of marine vessels, headquartered in Oslo, Norway—offers this description of modern-day Caribbean pirates that prey on yachts and other sea craft in the region.

> The pirates and raiders of previous centuries have been replaced by a modern variety every bit as evil as the buccaneers and freebooters of earlier times. Their sins today run the gamut from pilferage to murder. . . . Today's pirate comes in a variety of disguises virtually indistinguishable from the good island citizen. . . . Patagonia shorts, Sebago deck shoes and Veruchia sunglasses have replaced the pirates' broadcloth baggy trousers and pocketless shirts. The old buccaneer's cutlass has been replaced by the cell phone and laptop computer. The experienced cruiser learns to take precautions against thefts and criminality that would amaze any resident of the Bronx. Every type of boat equipment is subject to theft, and there are threats to personal safety unheard of on the mainland. These risks are taken in stride and are managed with aplomb by the aristocratic of the Caribbean cruiser class.

Guy Matthews. "Modern Pirates of the Caribbean." The Cruising Lifestyle Series, Bluewater Insurance. www.bluewaterins.com/second/pirates.htm.

ship's name on the hull and replace it with a new one. Next, they reregister the vessel under the new name in a country that asks few questions. Soon, the original identity of the vessel vanishes, as it becomes a "phantom ship." The renamed ship is then used for new criminal activities or it is sold.

And what happens to the crews? Many are killed, tortured, set adrift on lifeboats, or marooned on deserted islands. According to hard-to-verify reports, some kidnapped crew members are kept permanently at sea, forced to work as perpetual slaves on phantom ships run by their masters, the pirates.

Investing in Piracy

A large investment is required to carry out the type of crimes at sea that are performed by third-level pirates. The total cost for hijacking and turning a commercial vessel into a phantom ship could run as much as three hundred thousand dollars, an amount that lesser pirates cannot afford. If all goes according to plan, a "business" investment in a large-scale piracy raid could earn pirates millions of dollars.

According to the *Economist* magazine, much of this investment money comes from criminal organizations in countries such as Lebanon and Kenya. However, some of the top Somalian pirate gangs are now so prosperous from waging piracy that they can finance their own attacks. A few Somalian pirate gangs reportedly have developed their own stock market and invited others to invest in the profit-making activities. In recent years as many as seventy-two of these pirate-run maritime companies in Somalia were reportedly pooling their resources, such as weapons, boats, and tracking equipment, to finance ship hijackings. In return, "investors" receive a percentage of the ill-gotten gains from pirate raids.

Investments alone do not guarantee the success of a pirate raid. Because hijacking a large ship is so costly, dangerous, and complicated to carry out, it seems unlikely that the act could be executed by pirates alone. Instead, such a large-scale task requires help from corrupt business personnel and government officials. "The financiers are the most important [participants] since they organize and plan the big shot operations and are able to pay running cost[s]," a Somalian pirate told Scott Carney, a writer for *Wired Magazine*. "Financiers always need to forge deals with traders, land cruiser owners, translators, business people to keep the supplies flowing during operations and manage the logistics. There is a long supply chain involved in every hijacking."[7]

Bolder Attempts

Heavy investment in piracy has paved the way for extremely large-scale attacks and an increasing number of hijackings of large seagoing vessels. On September 25, 2008, for instance, fifty pirates seized the MV *Faina,* a Belize-flagged and Ukrainian-managed ship, about 250 miles (402.3km) off the coast of Somalia. The ship was large enough to be transporting thirty-three Soviet-era military tanks, tank artillery shells, grenade launchers and small arms and ammunition to Kenya. During the successful hijacking, the captain of the *Faina* was reported to have died from a heart attack. After threatening to blow up the ship, the pirates received $3.2 million in ransom money. They released the ship five months later.

An even more daring attack took place on November 15, 2008, when Somalian pirates stunned the shipping industry by seizing the VLCC *Sirius Star* supertanker—the largest ship ever hijacked—which was transporting 2 billion gallons (7.57 million kL) of oil worth $100 million to the United States. This seizure took place 450 miles (724km) off the coast of Kenya. Pirates held the *Sirius Star* until they received a hefty ransom.

Reasons for the Upsurge in Modern Piracy

Why has there been a surge in maritime piracy in recent years? For one thing, a four-decade-long political and military rivalry known as the Cold War between the former Soviet Union and the United States, along with its allies, ended in the early 1990s. As hostilities ended the two superpowers reduced the size of the fleets that had once patrolled the major sea lanes. As a result less-powerful nations have had to rely more on their own navies to protect vessels in their territorial waters. However, many poor coastal nations, such as Somalia, cannot afford to provide this

In September 2008 the Belize tanker Faina *was seized by Somali pirates. The pirates received $3.2 million in ransom for the tanker.*

security. In addition, there has been an increase in sea traffic in recent years, as the world's human population continues to increase and nations boost their international trade.

Advances in technology also have been a boon to piracy. Advanced communication systems, such as mobile phones, satellite navigation systems, Global Positioning Systems (GPS), and very high frequency (VHF) ship-to-ship and ship-to-shore radios help pirates locate and track their victims. And sleek, fast, fiberglass and inflatable dinghies with powerful outboard motors also enable them to travel faster than ever before to overcome slow-moving ships.

Meanwhile pirates have benefitted from technological changes inside the shipping industry itself. Labor-saving machinery installed aboard ships, advances in radio communications, navigational and engine performance, along with GPS devices, electronic sea charts, and automatic identification systems have all combined to lessen the need for humans working on board. In

Instability Creates Opportunity

Pottengal Mukundan, director of the International Maritime Bureau (IMB), tells how the conditions for piracy—greed, lawlessness, and opportunity—are present in pirate-plagued Somalia:

> If you look at any of the hot spots of piracy today, you will find these conditions present. For example, in Somalia there is no national government or law enforcement infrastructure, no one for the victims to turn to for assistance, there is pov-

erty from the fighting and chaos in the country, and there is [shipping] traffic along the coastline. So, it's a combination of social conditions, economic conditions, and the way law enforcement is done that allows piracy to flourish.

Quoted in Daniel Sekulich. *Terror on the Seas: True Tales of Modern-Day Pirates.* New York: St. Martin's, 2009, p. 23.

fact, ship crew sizes have shrunk from about an average of 250 men per ship in 1860 to only 15 in 2000.

They may become even smaller in the future. "In view of the technical progress and shortage of qualified crews, Scandinavian countries advocate crews with just 6 men on certain routes,"[8] observes Volker Bertram, a senior project manager for the Shamburg Ship Model Basin—a shipbuilding research center in Germany. Bertram and other industry experts also suggest that one day soon totally unmanned cargo ships will sail the oceans, either self-guided by advanced computers, or by humans operating remote controls from land or nearby ships. Though reduced crew sizes save money for shipping companies, they also make vessels more vulnerable to pirate attacks. In addition, slower ship speeds, a result of rising fuel costs, make hijacking easier than ever before.

Peter Chalk, an analyst for the Rand Corporation, an American nonprofit research organization, thinks the rise of terrorism has also indirectly fueled the rise of modern piracy. In a speech to a congressional subcommittee in February 2009,

Chalk pointed out that antipiracy measures normally carried out by many governments have declined worldwide since the September 11, 2001, terrorist attacks on the United States. This is occurring, he says, because governments are saving revenue to fund increased spending on security measures for their citizens on land against acts of terrorism. "This has further reduced what in many cases are already limited resources for monitoring territorial waters,"[9] according to Chalk.

The Rand study suggests that lax security exists along many coasts and in ports, especially in Brazil, East Africa, and parts of Southeast Asia. Lack of money is only one reason for this situation. Corruption in governments and businesses is another. Pirates in many countries, according to the study, bribe government officials to provide them with information about ships, or to help get pirated cargoes into the black market.

ARMED, HIGH TECH, AND DANGEROUS

"For some of us, it is a bit hard to believe that gangs of pirates are able to attack large merchant vessels in the busiest shipping lanes in the world. But they are doing it, often and without mercy to the helpless crews who are frequently held hostage for large ransoms."—John Payne is a seaman and author of several nautical, boating, and marine-based books, including *Piracy Today: Fighting Villainy on the High Seas*

John C. Payne. *Piracy Today.* Dobbs Ferry, NY: Sheridan House, 2010, p 5.

Today's pirates are also dangerous and heavily armed because they can buy cheap, powerful weapons from around the world. They, along with terrorists and criminals of all sorts, can obtain them quickly and easily thanks to the growing number of transportation options—boats, ships, planes, highways, and huge trucks—that make it easier and quicker for gun dealers to send the weapons to their customers worldwide. "These munitions include everything from pistols, light/heavy caliber machine guns and automatic assault rifles to anti-ship mines, hand-held mortars and rocket-propelled grenades,"[10] says Chalk.

The Financial Incentive

Modern piracy, of course, is a way to make lots of money quickly. Piracy is estimated to have provided Somalian pirates with $238 million in earnings during 2010 alone. This financial incentive makes a pirate's life attractive to many poor people, who have few, if any, other ways of earning a living. Somalian pirates, in fact, reportedly can make more money in one week as a pirate than they could otherwise in an entire year of doing legitimate work. "Hijacking a ship and kidnapping the crew for ransom is a lucrative business in Somalia," says Burnett. "It is less risky than robbing a bank and more profitable than pulling up half-empty fishing nets."[11] In 2009 Somalian pirates demanded and received at least $20 million in ransom from shipping companies that were all too willing to pay what pirates demanded of them for the return of their cargoes, ships, and crews.

The slums of Djibouti, Somalia. Poverty and internal political strife have provided fertile breeding grounds for pirates in countries such as Somalia, Malaysia, and the Philippines.

The lure of money, however, does not tell the entire story. The main reason that piracy thrives in Somalia is that it is a troubled land where poverty and lawlessness reign, and foreigners exploit the situation. Poverty and political strife have also provided fertile grounds for piracy in the waters off Asian countries such as Malaysia, Singapore, and the Philippines.

Piracy as Protest

Not all modern pirates rob, kidnap, and kill. One group of international mariners, in fact, proudly flies a pirate flag while its members try to save lives and enforce international laws. Their ranks consist largely of volunteers from several countries who work on vessels belonging to the Sea Shepherd Conservation Society. Founded by Canadian Paul Watson, Sea Shepherd wages what the organization calls "interventions" and the cable television network *Animal Planet* describes as "whale wars."

These interventions are aggressive attempts by Sea Shepherd crews to stop Japanese ships from killing as many as a thousand whales a year in the Southern Ocean Whale Sanctuary off the coast of Antarctica. The antiwhaling activists have assaulted Japanese whaling ships, using tactics that include throwing stink bombs, fouling propeller props, and boarding the Japanese vessels. Critics claim the whale protesters are pirates, because they forcibly come aboard the whaling ships, endanger human life, and destroy private property on the open seas.

Japanese whalers have responded by blasting protesters with water hoses, activating ear-splitting sound devices, hurling metal objects, and even ramming a Sea Shepherd small craft. The Japanese government, meanwhile, denies Sea Shepherd's accusation that their whalers are doing something wrong, and it claims the country's ships are legally harvesting the huge mammals for "scientific research" to research the age, birthing rate, and diet of whales. Sea Shepherd bitterly disputes these claims and argues that the real mission of the Japanese ships is to harvest whales for consumption.

The daring actions taken by Watson and his crew on icy, dangerous seas have earned the group praise from some people and condemnation from others. In 2008 the International

Accusing Greenpeace Activists of Piracy

In a December 27, 2005, open letter, Hiroshi Hatanaka, director-general of Japan's Institute of Cetacean Research, to Junichi Sato, campaigns director for Greenpeace Japan, accuses the environmental group of piracy in the following quote.

> Since December 21 [2005], in spite of repeated warnings and requests to move away, your activists continue to approach the Nisshin-Maru and our other vessels. Your organization continues to put in danger the lives of your crews by trying to board our vessels. In short, these actions amount to piracy. [Such] actions put at risk . . . the lives of our crews as well. . . . Your Zodiac boats are coming in front of the harpoon. . . . The explosive grenade harpoon, . . . [and] the high-caliber rifle . . . renders the situation an extremely dangerous one. There is also the risk of your crews' entanglement in the harpoon rope. . . . Once the harpoon has hit the whale, the area surrounding the vessel becomes very hazardous. . . . An accident has already occurred . . . [during which] the crew of one of your Zodiac boats ignored our warnings, became entangled in the wire [of the harpoon] and capsized. Your boats . . . are creating a situation where, sooner or later, an accident involving serious injury or worse may happen. . . . Furthermore, any escalation of Greenpeace's violent activities would correspond to piracy as defined by Article 101 of the United Nations' Law of the Sea.

Hiroshi Hatanaka. "Open Letter to Greenpeace Japan." Undercurrents/Greenpeace, December 27, 2005. http://members.greenpeace.org/blog/staff_oceans/2005/.

Greenpeace activists in small boats maneuver between two Japanese whaling vessels in a protest against Japanese whaling practices.

Whaling Commission called upon the Sea Shepherd Conservation Society "to refrain from dangerous actions that jeopardise safety at sea, and on vessels and crews concerned to exercise restraint."[12]

Among Sea Shepherd's sharpest critics are some Japanese and Canadian government officials who go so far as to label Watson and his crews as terrorists. Watson, however, defiantly defends Sea Shepherd's roughshod methods, saying they are necessary to protect an endangered species. As he puts it, "The only terror being committed in these waters is the cruel and illegal slaughter of whales in violation of international conservation law."[13]

As Sea Shepherd confronts Japanese whalers, a very different form of piracy, one that nobody disputes as criminal, is under way in a much warmer part of the world.

THE MOST PIRATE-INFESTED WATERS OF THE WORLD

In the first decades of the twenty-first century, by far the highest incidence of piracy on earth is off the Somalian coast. There, 139 of the 445 actual or attempted piracy attacks in the open seas worldwide occurred in 2010, according to the International Maritime Bureau (IMB). By the end of 2010 Somalian pirates held twenty-eight vessels and 638 hostages.

Somalia is located along the Gulf of Aden, which links the Arabian and Red Seas and is one of the world's most important bodies of water. The Gulf of Aden forms a natural barrier between the Middle Eastern country of Yemen and Somalia. Its waters flow north into the Red Sea through the Bab el Mandeb Strait, which connects the Gulf of Aden to the Red Sea and provides a pathway to the open sea. Here, along 2,000 miles (321.8km) of coastline, travel tens of thousands of slow-moving ships transporting much of the world's oil, supplies for the hungry in Africa, and commodities and supplies for millions of people. Watching and waiting for them are thousands of armed Somalian pirates.

A History of Violence and Poverty

The roots of Somalia's piracy legacy lie in its turbulent recent past. Though this poor nation achieved independence from the United Kingdom a half century ago, it has remained a poverty-stricken land torn by strife ever since. Violence had long played a role in Somalian life, but it exploded to new levels in 1991 when regional leaders, or warlords, toppled the nation's government and laid waste to much of Mogadishu, the capital city. A year later U.S. troops arrived to restore order and deliver much-needed aid to the Somalian people. Their arrival, however, provoked the warlords, who unleashed armed gangs against the Americans. Bloody street fighting quickly ended in disaster and humiliation for the U.S. troops, who soon departed the war-torn country. This bitter story was dramatized by the 2001 motion picture *Blackhawk Down*.

In the early years of the twenty-first century, a weak national government struggled to govern the country from its headquarters in Mogadishu, but it has exerted little influence on outer regions dominated by warring clans and subclans. Often led by greedy, powerful, and sometimes vicious warlords, these clans fight one another for power, control, land, and wealth.

Nature also turned against the Somalian people in the form of severe drought, which by 2011 had led the country to the brink of humanitarian disaster, according to the United Nations. It continues to force many people to flee the interior of

Somali fishermen bring a catch ashore. Fishing has declined rapidly in Somalia, due to the threat of piracy and because of competition from foreign fishing boats.

the country and settle near the ocean. There, they have joined Somalia's longtime coastal communities and turned to fishing to stay alive.

But Somalia's coastal resources have not been able to meet the needs of the Somalis. The fishing industry began to falter after the country became a failed state (one that is unable to carry out the basic functions of government) in 1991. Without a stable, powerful, central government, Somalia turned into a free-for-all zone for many other countries. Soon, fleets of huge commercial trawlers arrived from Western Europe and as far away as Japan to illegally help themselves to Somalia's abundant fisheries. According to the United Nations Food and Agriculture Organization (FAO), about seven hundred foreign vessels illegally harvested fish in Somalian waters in 2005 alone. Many of those ships are also accused of using internationally banned small mesh nets that ensnare all kinds of marine life, not just commercial-size fish. In addition, they are suspected of having used illegal, sophisticated underwater lighting systems to extract huge catches. Altogether, the alien poachers may have plundered as much as $300 million worth of seafood from Somalia.

Because of the ongoing political strife, Somalis had no navy, coast guard, or police force powerful enough to protect its territorial waters from this encroachment. "Every government in the world is off our coasts," said a Somalian pirate interviewed by *Wired Magazine*'s Scott Carney. "What is left for us? Nine years ago [in 2000] everyone in this town was stable and earn[ed] enough income from fishing. Now there is nothing. We have no way to make a living. We had to defend ourselves. We became watchmen of our coasts and took up our duty to protect the country. Don't call us pirates. We are protectors."[14]

The foreigners did more than steal fish. According to a 2005 United Nations Environment Programme report, many foreign ships used Somalian waters as a vast garbage dump for radioactive uranium deposits and other dangerous waste materials. Lack of coastal security also meant that smugglers found it easy and lucrative to sneak illegal substances, such as weapons and drugs, into the country.

A Somalian Pirate Explains Himself

A Somalian pirate, known as Asad 'Booyah' Abdulahi, recently explained to reporters of the United Kingdom newspaper the *Guardian* how he became a pirate:

> I am 42 years old and have nine children. I am a boss with boats operating in the Gulf of Aden and the Indian Ocean. . . . I started to hijack these fishing boats in 1998. I did not have any special training but was not afraid. For our first captured ship we got $300,000. With the money we bought AK-47s and small speedboats. I don't know exactly how many ships I have captured since then but I think it is about 60. Sometimes when we are going to hijack a ship we face rough winds, and some of us get sick and some die.
>
> We give priority to ships from Europe because we get bigger ransoms. To get their attention we shoot near the ship. If it does not stop we use a rope ladder to get on board. We count the crew and find out their nationalities. After checking the cargo we ask the captain to phone the owner and say that have seized the ship and will keep it until the ransom is paid.

Interview by Xan Rice and Abdiqani Hassan. "'We consider ourselves heroes'—a Somali Pirate Speaks." *Guardian* (Manchester, UK), November 22, 2008. www.guardian.co.uk/world/2008/nov/22/piracy-somalia.

According to a common explanation of these events, Somalian fishermen took matters into their own hands and formed vigilante groups to defend their waters. Using names such as the National Volunteer Coastguard of Somalia and the Somali Marines, unofficial volunteer coast guard units took to the sea and confronted the foreign ships. Using strong-arm methods, the vigilantes succeeded in chasing away many of the intruders. Many of those who remained were forced to pay a "duty" to fish or dump their foul wastes into Somalian waters.

Fisheries on the Rebound

These actions may have had an impact. By early 2010 fishermen from Kenya—Somalia's southeastern neighbor—reported that foreign trawlers had largely disappeared and the fish "which were once nearly depleted from overfishing" had returned. "There is a lot of fish now. . . . There is more fish than people can actually use because the international fishermen have been scared away by the pirates,"[15] says Athman Seif, the director of the Malindi Marine Association, which monitors the seafood industry on Kenya's Malindi coast.

However, many of Somalia's coast guard volunteers have not returned to fishing. Many discovered that harassing passing ships is more profitable. A four-month "fishing license" imposed on foreign ships, for example, brings Somalian "coast guards" up to thirty thousand dollars, according to some estimates. In addition, under the guise of protecting their country's waters, many former Somalian fishermen began preying on foreign ships. With the fishermen resorting to violence and force, it was only a matter of time until they became pirates. So many Somalis resorted to this criminal undertaking that Somalia's northeastern coastal state, Puntland, soon became the piracy kingdom of the world.

Somalia's Brand of Modern Piracy

Because piracy is so profitable, Somalia's sea coasts now teem with a wide range of pirates. While many of its lowest level pirates prey on small fishing boats and steal whatever they can, better organized gangs demand money from the owners of nearby boats and ships. In return, the pirates offer to protect them from harm. However, it is the pirates themselves who pose the real dangers to their "customers," if they do not pay for the so-called protection.

Somalia's most powerful, lucrative, and increasingly common form of piracy since 2005 involves gangs that seize and hijack large ships and luxury yachts, holding the vessels and the people aboard them for ransom. According to the IMB, Somalian pirates were responsible for 92 percent of all reported ship seizures in the world by the end of 2010.

Until a violent incident in February 2011, in which Somalian pirates killed four American passengers on a yacht, Somalian pirates had generally refrained from killing their captives. They were, however, often excited, nervous, and agitated while they carried out their criminal acts, in part, because they chewed the dried leaves of a local plant called khat, which works as a stimulant. With dangerous weapons in the hands of young, drugged pirates in extremely tense situations, violent incidents seemed inevitable.

MAJOR NAVAL POWERS STYMIED

"It's remarkable that 28 nations combining their maritime forces together in the Gulf of Aden have not been able to defeat this challenge."—Admiral Robert Willard, head of the Pacific Command, as told to the Asia Society in Washington, D.C., February 2011

Quoted in Shaun Tandon. "Somali Pirates Heading to Asia: US." Yahoo! News, February 17, 2011. http://news.yahoo.com/s/afp/20110217/pl_afp/usmilitarypiracy somaliamaldives.

Because so many pirates began to lurk along the Somalian coast, they often competed for ships they wished to attack. In January 2010, for example, a pirate gang in speedboats hijacked the *Maran Centaurus,* a supertanker transporting $150-million-worth of crude oil 800 miles (1287km) off the Somalian coast. The Somalian marauders demanded $5.5 million in ransom, which the ship's owner agreed to pay. However, just before the money arrived by plane for drop-off, another gang arrived and began firing at the pirates aboard the Greek-flagged ship. Soon, a blazing shoot-out between the rival pirates groups was under way. The gunfire was dangerous in itself, but making the situation even more hazardous were the 2 million gallons (7570kL) of combustible oil inside the tanker. Conditions, in fact, are so hazardous on oil tankers, such as the *Maran Centaurus,* that a mere spark can explode the ship. For that reason, no smoking or cell phone use is allowed on board at any time.

Finally, the pirates aboard the *Maran Centaurus* grew so worried about their safety that they called for help from the European Union's antipiracy naval force that patrolled for pirates not far away. Soon, two military helicopters arrived and frightened off the attacking pirates, and possibly prevented a catastrophe.

Afterwards, ransom money was parachuted from a passing plane to the hijackers, and the siege came to an end.

Blood Money

Although many of those who live in Somalia's coastal villages deplore the ongoing piracy, others turn a blind eye because it brings much needed wealth to many towns and villages that not long ago were on the edge of collapse. Somalian pirates, in fact, enjoy an elevated status in many Puntland communities because their neighbors consider them Robin Hood–like heroes that take from the rich and give to the needy.

Most of the bandits are young men between the ages of twenty and thirty-five. Their new wealth allows them to spend lavishly, build big homes, buy cars, and marry beautiful girls, often more than one. They "have money; they have power and they are getting stronger every day,"[16] Abdi Farah Jura, a resident of Puntland, recently told a reporter for the British Broadcasting Corporation (BBC).

The majority of Somali pirates are young men between the ages of twenty and thirty-five. Most come from poverty and therefore are lured by the idea of gaining riches, even through illegal means.

Eyewitness to Somalia's Pirate Coast

The following passage, taken from an article by Scottish journalist David Pratt, provides a firsthand look at Merka, the coastal pirate capital of Somalia.

It was almost dusk and the sun was sinking on the horizon. A few hundred yards offshore, the freighter that had earlier dropped anchor was swarming with local Somali men. The ship's crew, however, were nowhere to be seen.

Some of the Somalis carried Kalashnikovs [AK-47 assault rifles] and stood guard, while others, like worker ants, busied themselves loading the ship's cargo on to barges that were then hauled to the beach by relays of sweating men pulling on ropes.

Noticing my curiosity, one of the staff at the tumbledown guesthouse in the port town of Merka where I was staying decided to offer an explanation as to what I was witnessing.

"Our coastguards," he said with a mischievous grin. "Some of them used to be fishermen, but today, with the war and no law or government, they have a more profitable catch," nodding towards the rusting hulk sitting offshore.

Until that moment, nothing I'd seen had struck me as being out of the ordinary.

David Pratt. "Pirates of the 21st Century." *Herald* (Glasgow, Scotland), November 22, 2008. www.herald scotland.com/pirates-of-the-21st-century-1.827551.

Fierce critics of Somalian piracy, including many Somalis, acknowledge the connection between lawlessness, poverty, and the rise of piracy. Nonetheless, they condemn what is happening in the Gulf of Aden, because it is criminal and morally wrong. "The problem of overfishing has always been there, in the Caribbean, Latin America and the Indian Ocean. It doesn't mean that you take the law into your own hands,"[17] complains Abdillahi Mohamed Duale, the foreign minister of Somaliland, an autonomous, or self-ruled, state that declared its independence from Somalia in 1991.

Many observers of the situation in Somalia reject the idea that Somalian pirates have no economic alternatives. Instead, say these critics, many of the pirates are young thugs, dazzled by a chance to get wealth rapidly, who have fallen under the spell of landlocked warlords that have expanded their criminal activities to the Gulf of Aden. Critics also reject claims that Somalian pirates are merely protecting their coasts by "taxing" foreigners. If so, say critics, why are many of these same pirates harming their own people by repeatedly attacking international ships carrying food and medicine to tens of thousands of poor, hungry Somalis?

Such was the case on June 27, 2005, when Somalian pirates captured the MV *Semlow*, a chartered ship that departed the Kenyan port of Mombasa as part of the United Nations World Food Programme to help the victims of a tsunami that had swept over the Indian Ocean. The ship had entered Somalia with 850 tons (771 metric tons) of food for the country's hungry people when it was attacked by pirates. The pirates held the crew captive for eight weeks, demanding five hundred thousand dollars for their release. The ransom, however, was never paid. Finally, the pirates abandoned the hijacked ship along with its crew, and raided another vessel, the Egyptian-flagged MV *Ibn Batouta*.

Somalis Rise Up Against Piracy

Many Somalis who strongly oppose the widespread piracy in their country are businessmen who fear that the maritime crimes create an image of their country as being so backward, dangerous, and unmanageable that it cannot be trusted by other nations. They suspect that many foreigners would not wish to invest in such a country, or to provide food and relief supplies. In addition, many Somalis understand all too well that in lands ruled by force, pirates who become rich and powerful are likely one day to take control of local coastal villages.

Many of Somalia's religious leaders—primarily Muslims, followers of Islam—also profess outrage against piracy, especially if it is carried out against a ship from a Muslim nation. They insist that piracy violates Islamic teachings against murder and theft and that pirates should suffer severe punishments for these acts. In addition, they consider the pirates' habits of chewing khat, smoking hashish, and drinking alcohol as un-Islamic.

These critics do more than complain. Many Islamic militants, in fact, have taken action against local pirates. This became clear in 2006 when one armed group known as the Islamic Courts Union (ICU)—determined to impose a government steeped in Islamic law—took over the Somalian government. During the brief period in which the ICU ruled much of Somalia, it stamped out piracy.

This mopping-up action, however, did not last long. The United States, along with several other nations in Western Europe, had watched the rise of the ICU with alarm. Ever since the September 11, 2001, terrorist attacks on the United States, these powers have been wary of militant Muslims gaining political power anywhere in the world. Fearful that the ICU would

Gunmen protect leaders of the Islamic Courts Union as they install a new court in Balad, Somalia, in 2006. While the union was in power, it stamped out piracy in the areas under its control.

forge ties with al Qaeda—the terrorist organization responsible for the 9/11 attacks—the United States backed a 2007 invasion by neighboring Ethiopia that drove the ICU from power.

That support may be proving counterproductive. Anarchy returned to the country after the ICU fell from power, and all too soon Somalian pirates were back in action. Today some international affairs experts believe that the renewed lawlessness in Somalia may actually attract al Qaeda recruiters who are eager to exploit the fear and hopelessness in Somalian society.

PIRACY STILL UNCHECKED

"As long as pirates continue harassing shipping; endangering the critical delivery of humanitarian aid carried by ships chartered by the World Food Programme; and hijacking ships and seafarers, we are neither proud of, nor content with, the results achieved so far."—Efthimios E. Mitropoulos, secretary-general of the International Maritime Organization

Efthimios E. Mitropoulos. "Piracy: Orchestrating the Response," February 3, 2011. www.imo.org/MediaCentre/SecretaryGeneral/SpeechesByTheSecretaryGeneral/Pages/piracyactionplanlaunch.aspx.

However, other Islamic groups in Somalia still crack down on pirates whenever they can. In fact, their punishment is often so brutal that in 2008 the British Foreign Office caused controversy in Great Britain and elsewhere by announcing that any Somalian pirates who faced beheading or having their hands chopped off by an Islamic court for their pirating crimes could legally seek asylum in Great Britain on the grounds that their human rights were at risk.

Is Piracy at the Core of Somalian Culture?

Some observers of Somalian life think that piracy is part of a much larger network of corruption that runs rampant throughout Somalian culture. Extortion, bribery, and ransom demands have been a part of daily life in the country for centuries. In fact, many victims of Somalian piracy today may be those who fail to

U.S. Navy Officers' Description of Somalian Pirates

"I spoke recently with several U.S. Navy officers who had been involved in anti-piracy operations off Somalia, and who had interviewed captured pirates," writes Robert D. Kaplan, author and foreign affairs expert.

The officers told me that Somali pirate confederations consist of cells of ten men, with each cell distributed among three skiffs. The skiffs are usually old, ratty, and roach-infested, and made of unpainted, decaying wood or fiberglass. A typical pirate cell goes into the open ocean for three weeks at a time, navigating by the stars. The pirates come equipped with drinking water, gasoline for their single-engine outboards, grappling hooks, short ladders, knives, AK-47 assault rifles, and rocket-propelled grenades. They bring millet and qat (the local narcotic of choice), and they use lines and nets to catch fish, which they eat raw. One captured pirate skiff held a hunk of shark meat so tough it had teeth marks all over it. With no shade and only a limited amount of water, their existence on the high seas is painfully rugged.

Robert D. Kaplan. "The Chilling Innocence of Piracy." *Atlantic,* October 1, 2008. http://thecurrent.theatlantic.com/archives/2008/10/pirates.php.

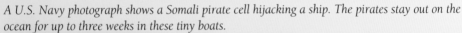

A U.S. Navy photograph shows a Somali pirate cell hijacking a ship. The pirates stay out on the ocean for up to three weeks in these tiny boats.

pay off government officials and corrupt warlords who control the country's transportation routes. Observes Iqbal Jhazbhay, an expert on Somalia at the University of South Africa, "The pirates ran roadblocks in the past, which were fleecing people as a form of taxation. Now they've seen the opportunities on the high seas."[18]

Michael Sparrow, the director of the local chapter of the Mission to Seafarers, an Anglican Church–backed outreach program for sailors in the city of Mombasa in neighboring Kenya, explains: "No one trades up there without paying bribes; it is what makes the difference between a safe voyage and a hijacking."[19] According to Sparrow, warlords control the ports, the fishing waters, and the sea lanes. It does not matter, he says, what kind of cargo is on board a ship, because "nothing gets into or out of Somalia, nothing passes by its coast, without money being paid."[20] And if a shipping company does not pay, he says, it is targeted by pirates who work for the warlords.

Despite the opposition of Muslim leaders and condemnation from around the world, piracy shows no sign of disappearing in the Gulf of Aden. It remains the best economic hope and perhaps even provides a form of coastal security for many Somalis. "We don't see the hijacking as a criminal act but as a road tax because we have no central government to control our sea," says Asad 'Booyah' Abdulahi, a Somalian pirate. "We will not stop until we have a central government that can control our sea."[21]

Until Somalia establishes a stable and effective government, the ongoing troubles will most likely continue to fuel piracy. Meanwhile, other criminal hot zones around the world are also swarming with pirates.

Piracy Hot Spots Around the World

Although Somalian pirates are expected to launch the lion's share of pirate attacks for years to come, maritime criminals will plague the shipping industry in other hot spots as well, ranging from Africa to Asia to the Caribbean islands to the coasts of South America. Though assaults in these hot spots vary in frequency, scale, style, and degree of violence, they all disrupt and damage international trade and jeopardize and take human life. One of the most violent of these hot spots lies on the opposite side of the continent from Somalia.

Nigerian Piracy: Fighting Foreign Oil Companies with Piracy?

Nigeria is a coastal country located near the equator on the western side of Africa. Although an oil-rich nation, Nigeria is torn by corruption and religious strife that hamper its economic and political development. The Nigerian government is therefore poorly equipped to defend a stretch of coastline between its oil-rich states of Bayelsa and Delta. In addition, an estimated 3,014 creeks lead to the ocean along this coastal expanse, making it easy for lawbreakers or rebels to hide and travel.

Here, along the Gulf of Guinea, which Nigeria shares with neighboring countries, pirates are waging war against foreign oil industries. Although pirate attacks have dropped from forty in 2008 to nineteen in 2010, the International Maritime Bureau (IMB) states that many attacks probably go unreported. In addition, the pirate-reporting organization warns that Nigerian pirates are armed, violent and aggressive, and that all waters off Nigeria are risky.

Nigerian militants patrol the Niger Delta region. The militants continuously attack oil company facilities and kidnap employees in the oil-rich region.

Most pirate attacks occur around the capital, Lagos, and along the southern Niger Delta. Clashes with government forces are frequent and the Nigerian Navy, antiquated and ill equipped, often finds itself outmanned by local pirates.

Piracy in Nigeria, as in Somalia, is bred in poverty, anger, and political unrest. Freed from British colonial rule for about fifty years, Africa's most populous country has seen a series of dictatorships rise and fall. As a result of these political upheavals, corruption is rife in the national government. Making matters worse, most Nigerians have not enjoyed the economic benefits from the massive drilling and pumping of their nation's oil fields. There is a widespread belief in the country that foreign oil companies that lease Nigerian oil fields, such as BP and Royal Dutch Shell, along with a small number of Nigerian government officials, reap most of the riches from the exploitation of their nation's oil reserves.

Instead of wealth, most Nigerians are confronted by the harmful effects of the oil industry. Their rivers and farmlands have been contaminated from oil spills and leaks that result from drilling and piping operations, and much of this pollution is allegedly left unattended by company and government officials. Many Nigerians claim the damage from pollution is so pervasive and destructive that they can no longer fish or farm for a living.

Several militant groups have formed in recent years in response to these perceived injustices and have announced that they must take matters into their own hands to protect their country from further plundering and exploitation. One of these militant political groups is known as the Movement for the Emancipation of the Niger Delta (MEND). The organization's leaders insist that their members have had to resort to drastic measures to stand up for poor, powerless Nigerians unable to protect their country's resources and environment. To that end, MEND demands that the Nigerian government cease exporting oil, turn over control of oil production to local people, and seek compensation for damages caused by oil spills and contamination of the mangroves, creeks, swamps, and fields of the Niger Delta.

Violent Politics in Nigerian Piracy

MEND, along with other insurgents, gangs, and soldiers of fortune, has turned to piracy as one way of waging war against foreign oil producers. In recent years, the group has stolen oil supplies, kidnapped oil company executives and workers, planted car bombs, and seized ships. Their speedboats have also made attacks along Nigeria's coasts. Such was the case with a successful 2008 armed robbery of Port Harcourt's harbor area's First Bank of Nigeria, which was transferring $2.5 million worth of funds. MEND's attacks have proved so successful that at times they have disrupted the flow of oil going to market by as much as 30 percent.

Nigerian pirate attacks are not always successful. For example, in September 2010 one group of pirates armed with rifles fought a losing battle with Nigerian naval forces to capture an offshore oil rig. Despite their defeat, the pirates managed to kidnap three French oil industry employees as they departed the area.

Facing Pirates Alone

In John S. Burnett's *Dangerous Waters: Modern Piracy and Terror on the High Seas,* the author, an experienced sailor, provides this description of his personal experience of piracy, when three pirates boarded his 32-foot sloop (9.7m) one night off the coast of Singapore City.

> We stood facing each other. No one had ever pointed a loaded gun at me before and staring into the barrels, I became weak with fear. . . . The older boy massaged the trigger with his forefinger. He jabbed the barrel of his rifle into my ribs silently egging, taunting, challenging. His deep-set eyes, like black glass marbles, drilled into mine with . . . [unexplainable] anger. I stood before him with my teeth clenched, unflinch-
> ing, staring into those depthless sockets. He poked my gut, then jabbed harder, testing the tenderness of the meat. Emboldened, he jabbed again as if the barrel of his gun were a bayonet. The hard metal felt like a dull knife. . . . I was close . . . one little push and he'd be overboard. I was about to do something really stupid. The older man's squeaky voice cut like a razor. "Money! You MONEY!" he said. . . . As I turned, the surly youth slammed the butt of his rifle against the back of my head.

John S. Burnett. *Dangerous Waters: Modern Piracy and Terror on the High Seas.* New York: Dutton Penguin, 2002, pp. 5–6.

Regardless of their motives, MEND pirates are considered criminals by Nigerian government officials and many independent observers around the world. Many Nigerians, however, view the insurgents and other like-minded gangs as heroes who try to right the wrongs inflicted on their society by outsiders. Other Nigerians deny that patriotism motivates the militants. Instead, they suspect that groups like MEND only pretend to be protectors to disguise their true intention of making themselves rich.

Indonesia and the Malacca Strait

Until recently another piracy hot spot has been the Strait of Malacca, a narrow 500-mile (804.6km) stretch of water in Southeast

Asia that separates the country of Malaysia from the Indonesian island of Sumatra. By connecting the Indian and Pacific Oceans and providing a route between the economies of Asia and Europe, the Malacca Strait has played an important role in global trade for centuries. Its maritime importance lives on today. An estimated 40 percent of the world's trade passes through this famous passageway every year, transported by some sixty thousand ships.

The rich bounty being transported through the strait attracts pirates in modern times, as it has for centuries. The geography of the Malacca Strait also invites piracy. For one thing, the strait is narrow. In fact, at one point it is only 1.7 miles (2.7km) wide. This "chokepoint" makes it relatively easy for sea robbers to pounce on almost any of the two hundred large, slow-moving vessels laden with oil, gas, and a vast assortment of manufactured goods that pass by each day. Thousands of islands, along with numerous tropical coves, creeks, and mangrove swamps provide hiding places for pirates in areas surrounding the strait. When darkness descends, many pirates roar off into the strait in their speed boats to seize cargo and container ships.

TOO SCARED TO TRAVEL

"A number of ships will not go through piracy zones right now. . . . They'll actually reroute around the coast of Africa, via the Cape of Good Hope. Costs there are about $2.4 to $3 billion per year."
—Anna Bowden, author of a piracy report for the Colorado-based think tank One Earth Future

Quoted in Voice of America. "Study: Piracy Cost World Up to $12 Billion Annually," January 14, 2011. www.voanews.com/english/news/africa/Study-Piracy-Costs-World-up-to-12-Billion-Annually-113609239.html.

Some pirates in the region are willing to rob and extort money from their neighbors who live and work along the coast. Local fishermen complain that these pirates force them to buy "safe fishing certificates" or face violent retribution.

Many pirates in Indonesia, like their counterparts elsewhere in the world, took up a life of crime at sea to provide a livelihood during a time of crisis. Such is the case with many of the pirates who live in Aceh, a territory located at the western tip of Sumatra. Up until 2005 militant insurgents in the region had fought the Indonesian military for more than thirty years to create an independent Islamic homeland. This bloody struggle, however, accomplished little more than impoverishing the local population and leaving many with few alternatives to piracy.

Piracy is an old tradition in the Malacca Straits. As *Time* magazine writer Alex Perry observed in 2001, "As they have for centuries, countless groups operate throughout the vast archipelago, raiding ships from Malaysia and the Philippines in the north to the waters off Australia in the south."[22] This situation, however, would change in the early years of the twenty-first century.

Patrolling the Strait

For years, it had been left up to the government of Malaysia alone—which is more prosperous than neighboring Sumatra—to send patrol boats out into the Malacca Strait to confront and catch pirates. Malaysian law enforcement officials complained that they were unable to carry out their antipiracy missions because they lacked resources and did not receive enough help from their neighbors.

By 2004, however, the three major political powers in the region—Malaysia, Indonesia, and Singapore—all realized that piracy had severely damaged their respective economies and presented an ongoing threat to human lives and international commerce. Soon government officials from the three nations agreed to work together to end the threat. That decision came none too soon. By 2005 the insurance company Lloyds of London listed the strait as the worst stretch of piracy in the world and raised insurance rates dramatically there.

The antipiracy plan worked out by the three Asian nations included using military-trained sea patrols and airplanes that spotted pirates. The nations also agreed to share intelligence gathered on pirates and to improve communications among their military and law enforcement agencies. However, when it became clear that Indonesia was unable—or unwilling—to do its full share to patrol the waterway, India stepped in to help and dispatched ships from its own naval fleet to the area. Thailand also provided vessels. This crackdown coincided with a cease-fire in Aceh, along with the lingering effects from a catastroph-ic 2004 tsunami that wiped out many pirates and their boats. When the number of pirate attacks fell to fifteen in 2008, the IMB felt compelled to describe the Strait of Malacca as a bright spot in the battle against pirates—one of the few in the world.

Malaysian police confront a pirate onboard a hijacked ship in the Malacca Strait. A number of nations are working together in an effort to eliminate piracy.

This achievement stands out even more when it is noted that at the same time the number of reported pirate attacks worldwide was at an all-time high. However, the IMB's 2011 quarterly report still advises ships' captains in the region to maintain strict antipiracy watch while under way in the straits.

Piracy in Asia

The impact of the antipiracy crackdown ends when ships sail past the last of the antipirate patrol boats. Eastbound vessels today still face threats of piracy as they pass by Singapore on the Malacca Strait. From here they move into a zone with a history of violent pirate attacks. "Located on the eastern side of the strait, the South China Sea is a violent, unregulated no-man's land, the private game reserve of organized crime. It is in these international waters that the hulking beasts of the sea like the *Petro Ranger* are hunted down,"[23] author John Burnett wrote in 2002.

The hijacking of the *Petro Ranger* took place in April 1998. The Singapore-registered ship was carrying 9,600 tons (8,708 metric tons) of diesel and 1,200 tons (1,088 metric tons) of jet fuel when it was boarded by pirates wearing ski masks off the Singapore coast. After ordering the crew to paint over the old ship name with a new one, the MV *Wily*, the pirates replaced the Singapore flag with one from Honduras. Two days later, the hijacked ship rendezvoused with two other ships at sea that siphoned off half of the $2.3 million worth of fuel the *Petro Ranger* was carrying. A few days later Chinese coast guard authorities stopped the hijacked ship and mistaking the pirates for the real crew, escorted the ship to the harbor of Hankow in China for a routine inspection.

Meanwhile, tied up below, the ship's captain, Australian Ken Blyth, and his crew waited in terror. They feared that once the ship was cleared for departure, the pirates might murder them. "All the pirates had to do was kill the crew and then go to another port, sell the ship or just get away,"[24] recalls Bangladeshi Mohieddin Ahmed Farooq, the *Petro Ranger*'s chief engineer.

Determined to avoid such a fate, Blyth and a Chinese-speaking crew member managed to escape later that night.

A Visit to Pirate Island

This section of a 2001 report from *Time* magazine correspondent Alex Perry gives a sample of what he discovered on Babi, a pirate-infested, slum-ridden island near Singapore.

The pirate king claims he has largely given up his old escapades when he and his crew would routinely hit 15 cargo ships on a moonless night for cash and whatever else they could carry. . . . Much more lucrative, and safer, is mercenary work. Nearly all the Babi pirates are *bajing loncat*, or jumping squirrels, men from Palembang in south Sumatra who over the centuries developed an unrivaled reputation for hijacking and robbery, on land or sea. The Babi pirates are the Elite, specialist raiders hired to steal mammoth 100-m, 10,000-ton ships and their entire cargo. For as little as $5,000, up to eight masked men will drive a speed-boat under a tanker's arched stern and scramble aboard using 20-m hooked bamboo poles, known as satang. After emptying the safe and taking whatever they find—computers, watches, refrigerators ("shopping," the pirate king shrugs)—they hand the ship over to a crew of professional seamen waiting in a second boat and leave—generally inside 10 minutes. "Same old work," says the pirate king, tapping the side of his head, "but now I'm using this." The men still carry machetes, cutlasses and homemade samurai-style swords like their forefathers before them. "You don't need guns," he smiles. "Indonesians are very skillful with knives."

Alex Perry. "Buccaneer Tales in the Pirates' Lair." *Time Asia*, August 20–27, 2001. www.time.com/time/asia/features/journey2001/pirates.html.

Avoiding their captors, they crept up to the bridge of the ship and convinced Chinese coastguardsmen who were keeping watch that the pirates were impostors and had hijacked the ship. The next morning, armed police boarded the *Petro Ranger* and arrested the pirates, who were later imprisoned for about a year without ever being charged with a crime. The police also seized Blyth and his crew that same morning and held them for several weeks before releasing them. Eventually, the *Petro Ranger* was returned to its rightful owner, Alan Chan's Petro Ships in Singapore. First, though, the Chinese confiscated the rest of the ship's fuel and kept it as "evidence."

Other victims of Asian piracy soon met a much worse outcome. In November of that same year one of the most brutal and inhumane attacks in the world of modern piracy took place against the Hong Kong–owned cargo ship MV *Chang Sheng* off the coast of Taiwan. According to Chinese reports, pirates allegedly dressed as Chinese antismuggling police boarded the ship, blindfolded the crew, beat them to death, and threw their bodies, strapped with weights, overboard. Afterward, the pirates sold the ship for three hundred thousand dollars.

The pirates failed to get away with their heinous crimes. Evidence of murder emerged when mutilated bodies of the slain sailors were hauled up in fishing nets. Chinese Communist

The view from a Chinese navy helicopter shows the Chinese navy escorting ships in the Gulf of Aden. China has executed numerous pirates.

authorities caught, sentenced, and executed the killers by firing squad. This all happened because the Chinese government was "eager to show that [it was] serious about the alarming rise in various types of crime, one of the most worrisome side effects of the free-market reforms introduced in the early 1980s,"[25] writes Bertil Lintner in *Blood Brothers: The Criminal Underworld of Asia*. In fact, Lintner adds, this crackdown may be necessary because piracy in China "is back with a vengeance after years of rigid communist rule."[26] Though Chinese officials have cracked down on maritime crime in recent years, pirate attacks have more than doubled in the South China Sea with thirty-one in 2010, up from thirteen in 2009.

PIRATES HIDING OUT

"Pirates are lying low [in Indonesia and Malaysia] because of aggressive patrols . . . but they're not detained or arrested—they'll rise up again once patrols stop."—Noel Choong, Piracy Reporting Centre

Quoted in Lucy Williamson. "Somalia Effect on Piracy in Asia." BBC News, April 29, 2009. http://news.bbc.co.uk/2/hi/8014334.stm.

Other Asian Hot Spots

China is not the only Asian country with piracy problems. Though antipiracy measures have reduced piracy in the Philippines in recent years, pirate attacks against ships at sea remain a problem along the coasts of Vietnam, Indonesia, and India.

Chittagong, Bangladesh's main seaport, also is hard-hit by pirates, most of whom attack the crews of anchored vessels. As much as 75 percent of piracy in the country, in fact, was carried out while ships were at port. Pirate attacks in Bangladesh increased from eighteen in 2009 to twenty-three in 2010. Twenty-one of these vessels were boarded by pirates wielding knives. According to Vivay Sakhuja, a scholar at the Institute of Southeast Asian Studies and a former Indian navy officer, the attacks

Local people carry the body of one of the Bangladeshi fishermen who were killed by pirates and then stuffed into their boat's ice chamber.

are often vicious. Pirates murdered fourteen fishermen during one harbor raid and stole fifty thousand dollars' worth of fish. During another assault, pirates heaved thirteen crew members off a fishing vessel. "In 2004," Sakhuja writes, "Bangladeshi police found the bodies of 16 fishermen in the ice chamber of their boat F.B. Kausara."[27]

South America and the Caribbean

Piracy also occurs in South America, including countries such as Peru, Brazil, Colombia, Costa Rica, Ecuador, and Venezuela. The IMB reports that most of the South American attacks had been carried out while the vessels were berthed in port or while at anchor.

Pirate Executions

In his book *Blood Brothers: The Criminal Underworld of Asia,* author Bertil Lintner provides this description of the Chinese execution of the convicted pirates who bludgeoned to death the crew of the MV *Chang Sheng* and threw their bodies overboard.

It was execution day in Shanwei, an isolated town on the rugged, pirate-infested coast of China's Guangdong province. Thirteen men, handcuffed and shackled, had already been herded into the town's courtroom on charges of piracy. They staggered out soon after with their fates sealed: death by firing squad. "Doomsday arrives for 'evil monsters' of the sea," declared the local authorities with medieval relish, although afterwards they mellowed somewhat and allowed the pirates to drink a large amount of wine, "to help take away the tension of being executed," as one official put it. Thousands of people gathered outside the courthouse for a glimpse of the damned men as they were led away to the execution grounds. By then, most of the pirates were profoundly drunk and singing loudly. . . . Jumping up and down in his rattling chains, Yang Jingtao, a 25-year-old pirate, led the chorus with a boisterous rendition of Ricky Martin's theme song for the 1998 World Cup, ironically called The Cup of Life:

Go, go, go!

Olé, olé, olé . . .

Before Yang and his fellow convicts had time to sober up, they were trucked away to an open field on the outskirts of Shanwei, forced to kneel in a row, and dispatched one by one by an executioner with a Kalashnikov—one bullet through the back of the head, one bullet through the heart. A coroner was on hand to certify the deaths. Then, in the Chinese tradition, the families were billed for the price of the bullets.

Bertil Lintner. *Blood Brothers: The Criminal Underworld of Asia.* New York: Palgrave MacMillan, 2003. Extract, Asia Pacific Media Services Ltd. www.asiapacificms.com/books/blood_brothers.php.

The Caribbean islands, once the haven of swashbuckling pirates of the seventeenth and eighteenth centuries, remains a theater of crime for pirates, though on a far different scale of criminality. "The most prevalent and well known [piracy] arises from the petty thieves, pilferers and the occasional dockside thug," writes Guy Matthews, an author of two handbooks on marine insurance. "These bottom feeders of the pirate economy prey on the Caribbean cruiser by creating traffic in stolen gear such as dinghies, outboard motors, and VHF radios."[28]

Because the nations of the world are becoming so interconnected through trade, travel, and communication, piracy's impact is felt almost everywhere, no matter where the crime occurs. And even as piracy flourishes, an international response is growing to tame the lawless seas.

PIRACY AND
THE LAW

In the twenty-first century, nations have been banding togeth-er to fight piracy. As they do, they must agree on how to set up consistent and fair ways to pursue, prosecute, and punish pi-rates. Finding such an arrangement is difficult because so much piracy occurs in the oceans and seas that belong to no single country. In addition, there are over two hundred countries in the world, each with its own customs, cultures, and national laws that govern the maritime crimes that take place in that na-tion's own territorial waters.

At the moment the best that the world community can do is to rely on the rules of international law, which is formed by agree-ments signed by participating nations. National laws generally deal with individuals, but international law focuses on relation-ships between governments, and there are inevitably problems in enacting and enforcing the compacts or treaties that nations make with one another. Not all of the nations in the world take part in creating international agreements, nor do all abide by them. In addition, it is hard, short of using military force, to make sovereign nations honor their commitments. Nonetheless in the contemporary fight against piracy, many nations are do-ing their best to find common ground. Their first step is to build consensus to create a foundation for antipiracy law.

Building on the Past

Laws against piracy are as old as maritime crime itself. More than two thousand years ago Roman statesman Marcus Tullius Cicero declared that under Roman law all pirates were *hostis humani generis*—enemies of the human race, a concept that

Defining Piracy

Many nations respond to piracy on the basis of their interpretation of rules established by the United Nations Law of the Sea Convention (UNCLOS), a few articles of which are excerpted below.

Article 101
Definition of piracy

Piracy consists of any of the following acts:

(a) any illegal acts of violence or detention, or any act of depredation, committed for private ends by the crew or the passengers of a private ship or a private aircraft, and directed:

    (i) on the high seas, against another ship or aircraft, or against persons or property on board such ship or aircraft;

    (ii) against a ship, aircraft, persons or property in a place outside the jurisdiction of any State;

(b) any act of voluntary participation in the operation of a ship or of an aircraft with knowledge of facts making it a pirate ship or aircraft;

(c) any act of inciting or of intentionally facilitating an act described in subparagraph (a) or (b).

Article 105
Seizure of a pirate ship or aircraft

On the high seas, or in any other place outside the jurisdiction of any State, every State may seize a pirate ship or aircraft, or a ship or aircraft taken by piracy and under the control of pirates, and arrest the persons and seize the property on board. . . .

Article 107
Ships and aircraft which are entitled to seize on account of piracy

A seizure on account of piracy may be carried out only by warships or military aircraft, or other ships or aircraft clearly marked and identifiable as being on government service and authorized to that effect.

United Nations Convention on the Law of the Sea of 10 December 1982. www.un.org/Depts/los/convention_agreements/texts/unclos/UNCLOS-TOC.htm. www.un.org/Depts/los/convention_agreements/texts/unclos/unclos_e.pdf.

still defines the way many people around the world view piracy. How to deal with pirates was also mentioned in the sixth-century legal codes of Byzantine emperor Justinian. Centuries later England's King John's Ordinance of 1201 established maritime laws. The thirteenth-century Consolat de Mar ("Consulate of the Sea") established temporary maritime laws for ship travel in the Mediterranean. In addition, the Hanseatic League, an association of hansas, or coastal trading cities, was created to promote profitable trading among cities along the coast of Northern Europe from the Baltic to the North Sea. This large organization provided antipiracy rules over a wide region. Various antipiracy measures were also taken in Asia and the Mideast in past centuries.

Ironically some of the nations that led the fight against modern piracy once sponsored their own version of high-seas looting, known as privateering. In the sixteenth century European monarchs expanded the centuries-old custom of issuing letters of marque—documents that gave private sea captains royal permission to attack, steal, and hijack vessels of enemy nations during wartime, as they struggled against one another for dominance in the New World. The United States also used privateers in the War of 1812 with Great Britain. Author Daniel Sekulich points out that the U.S. government had, in fact, issued so many letters of marque "that by the time the war ended in 1815, thousands of men were sailing the Atlantic in search of prizes and not a few were disappointed to hear peace had broken out."[29]

Soon, however, Americans and Europeans alike concluded that such lawlessness on the open seas was no longer tolerable. Human safety was not their only concern, however. By this time, the Industrial Revolution was well under way. This meant that a growing number of commercial ships laden with manufactured goods were traveling to foreign ports and needed protection from pirates or anyone else who stole cargo and valuables or who damaged ships or interrupted sea commerce. So, in 1856 diplomats from various maritime nations met in Paris, France, to sign an international agreement that officially renounced

The Dutch fleet, as part of the Hanseatic League's efforts against piracy, attacks and defeats the Barbary pirates in 1686.

privateering. Fifty-two nations signed the document, which effectively brought the practice to an end, although the United States was not one of them. Although privateering is not the same as piracy, because it is considered a wartime action, the agreement was nonetheless one of the first major international attempts to tame the lawless seas.

Updating Piracy Laws

It was not until the mid-twentieth century, however, that the global community finally agreed on an international definition of piracy. As described in the 1958 Geneva Convention on the High Seas, piracy is defined, in part, as: "any illegal acts of violence, detention or any act of depredation, committed for private ends by the crew."[30]

In 1982 international antipiracy law received a boost when more than 150 countries signed the United Nations Convention on the Law of the Sea (UNCLOS). This document defines piracy

Making Charges Stick

In the following news excerpt, Joel Morgan, minister of the Seychelles Republic, a cluster of islands in the Indian Ocean, tells the Sofia News Agency of his difficulty in prosecuting pirate suspects that his government sent back to Somalia.

The case of the 23 suspected pirates [in September 2009] which we deported to Somalia is very simple. . . . Faced with a lack of evidence to prosecute the suspected pirates we were forced to set them free. We are a state which respects international law, as well as the justice system of our republic and we had no other option but to release them. Other nations have also reacted in a similar manner when there is no evidence.

It is very difficult to prove actions of piracy. The court case which will take place in a few weeks time in Victoria will be an example of this, although we have strong evidence against the 11 suspected pirates we arrested in December. We are revising our laws on piracy in order to reflect the modern piracy problem more effectively.

Ivan Dikov. "Seychelles Minister Joel Morgan: Somali Pirates Damage Both Maritime Trade and Regional Stability." Novinite.com, Sofia (Bulgaria) News Agency, March 10, 2010. www.novinite.com/view_news.php?id=114068.

Pirates are captured off the Seychelles Islands by armed forces. The Seychelles government released the pirates, lacking the evidence necessary to prosecute them under current maritime law.

as illegal acts committed on the high seas for private ends. It goes on to state, "On the high seas, or in any other place outside the jurisdiction of any State, every State may seize a pirate ship or aircraft, or a ship or aircraft taken by piracy and under the control of pirates, and arrest the persons and seize the property on board."[31]

International Legal Problems

Meanwhile, international law allows any nation to enforce its own piracy laws, when one of its own ships is attacked by pirates on the open seas, where no single country has legal jurisdiction. Countries, of course, enforce their own piracy laws in their territorial waters. But how far out to sea do these territories stretch? Until 1980 the international community agreed that territorial waters extended 3 nautical miles (a nautical mile is approximately 6,076 feet or 1,852 meters) from a nation's shore. However, in 1980 it added another 9 nautical miles. Today, some coastal nations also claim an additional 200 miles (321.8km) of exclusive economic zone, an area in which the country maintains special rights for exploration and control of marine resources.

LAWS PROTECT PIRATES TOO

"There are laws against a private individual killing a private individual, even if they are perceived to be pirates. You can't go on the high seas, just like you can't go on the streets of London, and shoot people likely to do harm to you."—Tony Mason, secretary-general of the International Chamber of Shipping and International Shipping Federation

Quoted in Sandra Jontz. "Hired Guns Secure Ships, Stir Controversy." *Stars and Stripes*, European ed., February 15, 2010. www.stripes.com/article.asp?section=104&article=68039.

Most piracy takes place within the 12-mile (19.3km) territorial zone, where it is left to sovereign nations to enforce their own laws. But that does not always mean that pirates will be caught and prosecuted by local authorities. Many poor nations do not

In June 2009 the International Maritime Organization met in Seoul, South Korea, with representatives of thirty countries and ten international agencies in an effort to bring piracy laws up to date.

have the resources or the will to confront pirates operating in their territorial waters. Countries in turmoil, such as Somalia, lack strong governments with the authority, military power, and money to gather intelligence to pinpoint pirates' whereabouts, figure out their plans, and pursue them after they have committed crimes.

Because legal definitions vary from one nation to the next, there is a lack of consistency among nations in the worldwide fight against piracy. Countries disagree over whether some maritime crimes should be called piracy or some other crime. For example, some nations consider the hijacking of a cruise liner by passengers for political purposes an act of terrorism. Others consider certain acts as mutiny or war and not piracy. Disagreement also centers on other questions. Are a minimum of two ships required for an act of piracy? Must a pirate crew be nonmilitary? Is a motive of self-gain the only one that qualifies sea robbery as an act of piracy?

The 2005 Protocols to the UN Convention for the Suppression of Unlawful Acts Against the Safety of Maritime Navigation, approved by the International Maritime Organization (IMO), expanded a 1988 maritime code to include acts of maritime terrorism, such as acts that may be termed political piracy, which was not mentioned in the original agreement. Nonetheless, many observers think the current language in the resolution still allows too many legal loopholes and uncertainties that make it hard for nations to create a single international standard. Dutch lawyer and professor of international law Geert-Jan Knoops pointed to these uncertainties when he asked the Dutch parliament in 2009: "Do you perceive combating piracy primarily as a criminal law issue, or as part of the law of war? Is it a war against piracy, or do you qualify it as part of the ordinary law enforcement system?"[32] Many nations, along with the Netherlands, consider the pursuit of pirates to be an extension of criminal law. But some analysts wonder if the existence of highly weaponized modern pirates may soon force nations to rewrite their legal codes and adopt a more warlike response.

Problems of national jurisdiction (authority to administer justice and apply laws) also arise. Many international law experts believe the best policy is for any apprehended pirate suspects seized in international waters to be turned over to authorities of a coastal country in the region. So far, however, it remains difficult to convince any nation to accept these suspects.

Penalties for piracy vary, too. Some nations governed by Islamic law, or sharia, may require that judges sentence pirates to the death penalty. Great Britain, on the other hand, forbids capital punishment for any crime. U.S. law requires life in prison. In addition, judicial systems vary from one nation to the next. There are, for example, big differences in standards of guilt, rules of evidence, and whether pirate defendants will face a jury or a panel of judges.

Other Law Enforcement Concerns

There are also other concerns over law enforcement. Because so many nations are involved in maritime shipping, it is not easy to pinpoint who should prosecute suspected pirates. As author John Burnett points out,

Consider a typical case: a ship built in Japan, owned by a brass-plate company in Malta, controlled by an Italian, managed by a company in Cyprus, chartered by the French, skippered by a Norwegian, crewed by Indians, registered in Panama, financed by a British bank, carrying a cargo owned by a multinational oil company, is attacked while transiting an international waterway in Indonesian territory and arrested in the Philippines.[33]

A long-standing frustration for nations using military force against pirates on the open seas arises from an understanding among nations that no country may legally send in its navy to

On December 16, 2008, U.S. secretary of state Condoleezza Rice votes for UN Resolution 1851. It granted maritime nations the right to pursue Somalian pirates into Somalian territorial waters and even onto Somalian land if done in cooperation with the Somali government.

UNITED STATES

pursue pirates into the territorial waters of another country, even if the foreign warships are in hot pursuit; that is, closely following a fleeing ship that has crossed into territorial waters.

There is, however, one major exception to this rule. In 2008 the United Nations Security Council adopted a resolution that for the first time ever granted maritime nations the right to pursue pirates into Somalian territorial waters and even onto Somalian land, as long as the nations are cooperating with the Somalian government.

Human Rights

Another point of contention is whether all nations will observe the human rights of pirate suspects and grant them due process of law. As is the case with piracy laws, the interpretation of human rights varies from one country to the next.

THE RIGHT OF SELF PROTECTION

"A bank doesn't transport money without armed guards or an armored car, why should boats not be able to protect themselves?"—William Callahan of the maritime security firm Unitel

Quoted in Charlotte Sector. "Danger Adrift: Modern-Day Pirates Threaten More than the High Seas." ABC News International, November 14, 2005. http://abcnews.go.com/International/story?id=1300344.

Many international law experts worry that there may be some countries that will not prosecute pirate suspects fully or at all, because they fear having to grant them asylum—protection from arrest and removal to another country—when they finish their prison terms. There is also concern over whether pirate suspects can receive fair trials in underdeveloped nations that are too poor or unwilling to send witnesses to distant countries where the suspects are being prosecuted in court.

How to treat pirate suspects who are minors is another thorny issue. Many suspects now in detention are juveniles, under the age of eighteen. This causes international concern because not all countries have specially designated juvenile justice

Seven suspected Somali pirates sit in a Kenyan courtroom facing international piracy charges.

systems, which hold minors to a different standard of behavior than adults. "I would be very uncomfortable about the increased possibility of sending children to stand trial in a foreign jurisdiction. If you want to go down that route, you might as well send them to China where there is no messing about—pirates are simply executed,"[34] says Anthony Rogers, senior lecturer of law at City University London and director of the master of laws maritime law course in Piraeus, Greece.

An International Court

Some maritime law experts think that a permanent pirate court might solve many of these antipiracy issues. For a time the European Union (EU) had convinced Kenyan officials—as it negotiated with others in Seychelles and Tanzania—to set up special courts in their land to try piracy suspects captured in the Gulf of Aden. In return for Kenyan help, the EU invested $3 million in the African nation's judicial system. In September 2010, however, the Kenyan government canceled the deal, which had proven unpopular with Kenyans and hard to implement. Kenyan officials also complained that the EU's financial support was less than expected. Even if the Kenyan piracy courts had continued, many analysts wonder whether such courts' laws would provide the type of justice that satisfies all the concerns of multiple advanced countries. Turning pirate suspects over to a third party also raises legal doubts. International law generally allows only the arresting nation to prosecute captives.

With all these legal headaches, many nations do not even bother to prosecute pirate suspects that they have taken into custody. It is common practice for military authorities from many nations to disarm and then release pirates they have apprehended. Such actions, however, draw protest from other nations, who demand justice. As the world community grapples with such thorny legal issues, the harm caused by modern piracy shows no signs of letting up.

THE DAMAGING IMPACT OF PIRACY

Piracy causes extensive damage around the world, including a hefty impact on the finances of businesses and consumers worldwide. Stolen goods, hijacked ships, missed deadlines, and security measures to protect property and crew all increase the cost of doing business. The total annual cost for piracy now runs between $7 billion and $12 billion every year. These expenses are ultimately passed on to consumers in the form of higher prices.

One of the biggest costs comes from rising insurance rates for shippers. In fact, the rapid rise of piracy is the main reason for insurance rates going up 350 percent in recent years to cover commercial ships passing through the Gulf of Aden, and 1000 percent for kidnapping and ransom coverage, according to *Risk Management* magazine.

Insurance Headaches

As never before, piracy is causing insurance companies and the shipping industry to decide what kind of insurance is both affordable and sufficiently protects the crew, passengers, cargo, and ship against damages and loss. The most common type sold is hull, or marine, insurance, which protects against losses due to damage to the structure of the ship if it runs aground or collides into another ship or dock. Insurers also offer protection and indemnity (P&I) insurance for crew members if they are injured or killed while at work.

In response to the rise in piracy, marine insurance companies now offer new kinds of coverage. One of them is "ransom" insurance, which can cost as much as $150,000 for $2 million in payments to pirate kidnappers.

Annual Estimated Costs of Piracy

Cost Factor	Cost
Ransoms (excess costs)	$148 million
Insurance Premiums	$460 million to $3.2 billion
Re-routing Ships	$2.4 to 3 billion
Security Equipment	$363 million to $2.5 billion
Naval Forces	$2 billion
Prosecutions	$31 million
Antipiracy Organizations	$19.5 million
Cost to Regional Economies	$1.25 billion
Total Estimated Cost	**$7 to $12 billion per year**

Taken from: Oceans Beyond Piracy. *The Economic Cost of Piracy.* oceansbeyondpiracy.org/sites/default/files/documents_old/The_Economic_Cost_of_Piracy_Summary.pdf.

Insurance giants, such as Lloyd's of London, now view many pirate-infested regions as combat zones and require many of their customers to buy "war risk" policies for ships traveling into these waters. Such war risk policies generally cover ships that are damaged or destroyed by acts of not only war, but also terrorism, mutiny, and piracy.

All of these added costs have been a boon for maritime insurers. Shipowners now spend $400 million a year for insurance, according to *Forbes*, a publication specializing in international business and finance. On average, shippers must pay about twenty thousand dollars for extra insurance costs for each voyage. Big tankers venturing into dangerous pirate zones can expect to pay much more. Some spend up to one hundred thousand dollars per voyage for "war risk" and kidnapping and ransom insurance.

Loopholes

Having maritime insurance, however, does not always guarantee that shipping companies receive the compensation they expect when they file a claim for piracy losses. Some insurance

U.S. Secretary of State Explains Piracy Policy

This quote from Secretary of State Hillary Clinton's April 15, 2009, announcement outlines U.S. policy concerning maritime piracy.

The United States does not make concessions or ransom payments to pirates. . . . The solution to Somali piracy includes improved Somali capacity to police their own territory. Our envoy will work with other partners to help the Somalis assist us in cracking down on pirate bases and in decreasing incentives for young Somali men to engage in piracy.

Second, I'm calling for immediate meetings with our partners in the International Contact Group on Piracy to develop an expanded multinational response. . . . This is a huge expanse of ocean, four times the size of Texas, so we have to be able to work together to avoid the pirates. We also need to secure the release of ships currently being held and their crews, and explore tracking and freezing pirate assets.

Third, I've tasked a diplomatic team to engage with Somali Government officials . . . as well as regional leaders in Puntland. We will press these leaders to take action against pirates operating from bases within their territories.

And fourth . . . I have directed our team to work with shippers and the insurance industry to address gaps in their self-defense measures.

Hillary Rodham Clinton. "Announcement of Counter-Piracy Initiative." U.S. Department of State, Washington, DC, April 15, 2009. www.state.gov/secretary/rm/2009 a/04/121758.htm.

On April 15, 2011, U.S. secretary of state Hillary Clinton's announced the the U.S. position on maritime policy, which included the development of a multinational response to piracy, a policy of not paying ransom money to pirates, and other measures.

adjustors, for example, may balk at compensating a customer if a crew member with P&I insurance is injured when fighting terrorists, especially if a mariner used a military-grade weapon. They could reject the claim by arguing that war risk protection, and not P&I, was needed to cover armed conflict. Or, they may argue that the use of weapons by crew members during a pirate attack actually made the situation worse and that the damages are therefore not covered by any insurance policy.

Sometimes, disputes arise over cargo that is stolen by pirates but is later released. Often it cannot be delivered on time or the cargo may be too damaged to sell. Insurers and shippers then argue over which of them should suffer the loss.

Many maritime insurance policies contain large deductibles, which are set amounts that shipowners must pay out of their own pockets before their insurance companies are willing to compensate them for losses. Sometimes these deductibles are so large that the insurance policies prove to be almost useless.

PROTECT LIVES ABOVE ALL

"My job as a business owner and my job as the CEO of people who entrusted their lives to me, when they sign on to my ships, was to ensure that I would get them home to their families safely. . . . Their lives and their safety is my primary concern."—James Christodoulou, CEO of Industrial Shipping Enterprises, who paid pirates a ransom to release his crew when taken hostage on his company's tanker, the MV *Biscaglia*

Quoted in Melissa Block. "To Pay Ransom or Not to Pay Ransom." National Public Radio, April 11, 2009. www.npr.org/templates/story/story.php?storyId=102977470.

Legal loopholes found in some policies also may prevent shippers from recovering some of their losses from piracy. For instance, insurers may claim that crew members who were robbed by pirates were actually "mugged" and thus not entitled to coverage. There are also reports that some insurance companies avoid covering losses on ships that have been attacked at sea by claiming that civil war, riots, or terrorism were responsible for the misdeeds at sea, not piracy. There may be debate over whether an insurance policy is still in effect in an incident in which a ship's captain changes course to avoid pirates, but is attacked anyway. Because the ship's original route may have been a significant factor in determining the cost of the insurance policy, the insurance company may escape responsibility.

Maritime fraud is always on the minds of insurers. Not all missing cargoes are stolen by pirates. Some go missing because corrupt ship crews or shipping officials lie about a theft, sell the missing merchandise on the black market, and then seek compensation for the "losses" from an insurance company.

Finally, many shipping companies often lament that the better insured their ships are the more likely they are to be pirated. Sophisticated modern pirates, after all, often know which ships carry kidnapping and ransom insurance, which they hope to exploit when they hijack the ships.

Ransom Risks

Ransom payments deliver a whopping financial blow to shippers. "By the end of 2010, approximately $238 million was paid in ransoms to Somali pirates in that year alone,"[35] according to the Colorado-based think tank One Earth Future.

Whether to submit to pirates' ransom demands haunts the executive boards of many big companies. Not to pay may mean the loss of human lives and property. On the other hand, rewarding pirates for their crimes only invites more sea robbery and extortion.

Making payments to pirates is a dangerous and complicated matter. For one thing transporting money in boats, or by planes, to armed men who may be using narcotics is dangerous. There are also cases of pirates attacking boats carrying ransom money to other pirates.

Paying ransom may violate laws of the nations from which boats and planes that deliver money embark. In these cases the ransom payers may have to use stealth. Many governments do not allow insurance companies to pay such ransom payments directly to pirates. In April 2010, for example, U.S. president Barack Obama issued an executive order making it illegal for

Members of a Spanish fishing crew are free after a reported ransom payment of $3.5 million. Many shipping companies would rather pay ransoms than risk the lives of their crews and the loss of cargo.

anyone to pay ransom to Somalian pirates who have hijacked a ship or kidnapped crew members or passengers. The obvious intent of the order was to discourage piracy. But many in the shipping industry are confused by the president's action and concerned that they might be prosecuted by the United States for trying to save the lives of their employees and protect their property. Critics complain that the president's order also hampers shippers' ability to respond to a crisis. Marie-Louise Moller, spokesperson for the shipping giant A.P. Moller-Maersk, explains, "Taking away our ability to secure the safe release of our crew members and vessels could put us as an employer and ship owner in a very difficult position."[36] Insurance companies sometimes sidestep such prohibitions by using a third party—a security company, for example to deliver the payments to the pirates.

Negotiations with pirates can be an agonizingly long and slow process, sometimes taking months. In February 2010 Somalian pirates released the Taiwanese fishing vessel *Win Far 161* and its crew after receiving a ransom. The pirates had held the vessel and crew for ten months while the ransom was being negotiated. During that time the pirates used the trawler as a mother vessel to attack other ships. By the time the ordeal came to an end, three members of the original crew had died from malnutrition and neglect.

Lawsuit Worries

Adding to the woes of shipping companies are lawsuits filed against them as a result of piracy. Some of these actions come from business owners who do not receive shipments on time after a hijacking. Sometimes lawsuits are filed by the shipping company's own employees who claim they have injuries caused by pirates. On November 19, 2009, for instance, six crew members of the *Maersk Alabama*, which had been hijacked by Somalian pirates earlier in the year, brought suit against the ship's owner, the Waterman Steamship Corporation, seeking compensation for injuries they claimed they had suffered during the attack. The plaintiffs alleged that the company failed to take adequate safety precautions prior to sailing into a region of the sea riddled with pirate activity. Families of crew members killed by pirates have taken legal action against shipping companies as well.

PAYING RANSOM IS PART OF THE PROBLEM

"Part of the problem is that the number of companies, not countries, companies that are prepared to pay the ransoms as part of the price of doing business and clearly if they didn't pay the ransoms we'd be in a stronger position."—U.S. defense secretary Robert Gates

Quoted in Brent Lang. "Gates: Stop Paying Ransom to Pirates." CBSNews.com, April 17, 2009. www.cbsnews.com/8301-503544_162-4952864-503544.html.

In some cases shippers find it is cheaper to offer out-of-court cash settlements than to defend themselves. These payoffs, however, may shortchange the injured, especially those in poor nations who lack the resources to fight in court. According

The crew of the Maersk Alabama *after their rescue. Crew members brought suit against the ship's owner, the Waterman Steamship Corporation, seeking compensation for injuries they had suffered during the attack.*

to John Burnett, "In the Philippines a ship owner pays up to $50,000 to the family of a seafarer killed during a pirate attack. And the book is closed. It is cheaper than keeping a ship in port for weeks while local authorities, prodded by a seaman's family, investigate the crime."[37]

Lawsuits filed by passengers aboard luxury ocean liners attacked by pirates prove challenging to shipowners. As Jim Walker, a Miami, Florida–based attorney specializing in maritime issues, points out, "Shipping companies and cruise lines face liability when they do not take reasonable steps to protect their passengers and crew members. They are legally responsible when they fail to protect the guests and crew from risks which are known or reasonably foreseeable."[38]

The Cost of Justice

Shipping companies must consider what they should do with pirate suspects who are captured by their own crew members, or hired security guards. Among other concerns, they must also consider the cost of keeping pirate suspects on board one of their ships until the crew is able to turn them over to a military or law enforcement authority. They may face additional expenses, such as travel expenses for witnesses who must appear in court in a foreign country to testify against pirate suspects. In addition, many companies must take into consideration whether market delays from taking the time to report and pursue piracy complaints add to their losses from piracy. Such delays cause losses averaging between $1 million and 2 million per attack.

When all expenses are added up, many company officials decide it is simply cheaper and easier to let the pirates go free. This, however, may only make the problem worse.

Other Economic Costs

Piracy imposes yet other economic costs on the shippers. Their industry often must pay higher wages and offer greater benefits to attract crews willing to travel through pirate hot zones.

Some shippers have decided their best option is to avoid encountering piracy in the first place. So, they order their ships to undertake safer but longer voyages to get their cargoes to market. After the hijacking of the *Sirius Star*, for example, A.P. Moller-Maersk, Europe's largest shipping company, ordered its fifty oil tankers to avoid the Suez Canal in Egypt—an important waterway that connects the Mediterranean and Red Seas. Instead, company ships traveled a much longer journey around Africa's Cape of Good Hope.

Avoiding pirates, however, is costly. According to John C. Payne, author of *Piracy Today*, "An oil tanker on a voyage from Saudi Arabia to the United States would add around 2,500 nautical miles to the voyage at an annual increase in fuel costs of about $3.5 million."[39] Longer trips also require more operating expenses for shippers. It currently costs anywhere from ten thousand to one hundred thousand dollars per day to operate a ship at sea, depending on the size of the ship. In addition, Payne points out, the time-consuming trip means the ship will not make as many paying voyages as it would otherwise. However, there are advantages to taking the longer, safer routes. Shippers can avoid costly pirate insurance and, by not using the

After the oil tanker Sirius Star *(pictured) was hijacked, the ship's owner, A. P. Moller-Maersk, ordered its tankers to avoid pirates near the Suez Canal by traveling instead around Africa's Cape of Good Hope.*

Suez Canal, they do not have to pay the toll, which for a container ship averages six hundred thousand dollars for each trip.

Sometimes fear of pirates causes sea captains to veer away from pirate zones without first getting permission from their employers. In Mombasa one frightened sea captain told a reporter for London's *Independent*, "I don't tell my company exactly what route I will be taking. I don't want people to know where I am."[40]

Piracy's Other Damages

The money pirates bring to their villages often boosts the financial well-being of the villages' residents. However, it also causes damage. International companies, which may otherwise be attracted to places where wages are low and business regulations few, may avoid setting up factories in countries that cannot, or will not, adequately patrol their territorial waters. Thus, the poor countries least able to police their coasts stand to lose if foreign manufacturers and investors head for other lands where pirates are not a scourge.

Piracy is also costly to governments that are forced to dispatch armed and trained personnel aboard ships, helicopters, and planes to free hostages or to launch patrols in pirate hot zones. Not only do such efforts drive up military expenditures, they also sap defense resources from other areas in the world that may demand a military presence. Naval operations off the Somalian coast alone cost at least $2 billion annually. The expenses, of course, are passed on to taxpayers.

Piracy also takes a toll on human beings. Crew members and passengers who are victimized or brutalized by pirates often face lasting physical and psychological damages. A few even die; while some never return home. Many victims of piracy never go to sea again.

Seafarers are not the only victims. Many poor fishermen in communities along the world's shipping lanes continue to be robbed and sometimes murdered by the pirates. For all these unfortunate human beings, relief cannot come soon enough.

FIGHTING BACK

F ed up with piracy, many people around the world are fighting back. Among them are tormented fishermen who live near pirates. Sometimes frustration and fear push them to the boiling point, and they strike back with violence. Such was the case in December 2003, when Bangladeshi villagers, angered by the continuous attacks from local pirates against local fishermen, banded together and seized and lynched twenty-eight suspected pirates.

They did not lynch them all, however. Four who managed to escape soon launched new assaults against the fishermen. These men, too, were then hunted down by the enraged villagers and beaten to death.

Some Somalian Islamists and warlords have also taken matters into their own hands. In April 2009 the British Broadcasting Corporation (BBC) reported that antipirate militias had been set up by communities in Somalia's Puntland. Faarah Mohammed, one of the "security" committee leaders, told the BBC that these groups "decided to confront whatever was creating problems in their areas and particularly, the problems of the sea piracy. And eventually their effort led to the capture of three boats and 12 men with their weapons. One boat got away."[41]

New Ways to Deter Pirates

The shipping industry, for the most part, believes it is safer and cheaper for their ships' crews not to respond with violence when pirates attack. Instead, many companies are employing best practices to protect their ships and crews.

Captain Allan Breese, senior marine loss control consultant at Allianz Global Corporate & Specialty insurance company, notes that "there are plenty of small steps that ships can take to make themselves less accessible to pirates, and all vessels should consider using some of them. The majority of pirate attacks are opportunistic, so the better prepared the ship, captain and crew are to deal with piracy risk, the more likely they will be to overcome the problem."[42] Among these precautions are for crews to maintain a high state of alert for piracy, respond quickly according to a rehearsed plan when pirates are spotted, and increase ship speed when pursued.

Many shippers have been upgrading their onboard pirate deterrence responses by using electric fences with enough current to shock but not kill, washing pirates overboard with fire hoses, employing evasive steering maneuvers, using acoustic devices that emit ear-splitting signals, securing all entrances, and increasing cruising speeds to 18 knots (21 miles per hour, or 33kph) or more.

Such precautions proved useful on the morning of November 5, 2005, when a gang of Somalian pirates attacked the *Seabourn Spirit*, a 440-foot-long luxury cruise ship (134m) belonging to the Carnival Corporation, as it traveled from Egypt to Mombasa. The pirates appeared suddenly in boats and opened fire with

Many ships are using pirate deterrence methods. After coming under gunfire from pirates, the captain of the cruise ship Seabourn Spirit, *shown here, fought back by turning on a painful sound device and running over one of the pirate boats.*

AK-47 assault rifles. As bullets sprayed against the starboard side of the ship, its three hundred passengers took cover inside. The pirates even used a rocket-propelled grenade launcher that slammed a projectile into the side of the ship. At last, the captain of the *Seabourn Spirit* drove off the pirates by using a painful sound device and running over one of the pirate boats.

In April 2010 the crew of the cruise ship *Discovery* may have deterred Somalian pirates with another technique. They unfurled rolls of barbed wire off the ship's stern to prevent pirates from boarding the ship.

Another antipiracy trend in the shipping industry is to install "citadels" on ships where crew members can go during pirate attacks. Inside these enclosed, fortified areas, they can safeguard themselves while protecting the ship's engine and communications systems as they summon help. Citadels, however, are not a cure-all for piracy attacks. The North Atlantic Treaty Organization (NATO), which includes the United States, Canada, and many Western European nations, warns the shipping industry that citadels should be a part of the ship's overall package of antipiracy tools, not a replacement.

Despite claims that these nonviolent practices are successfully thwarting attacks, many piracy experts doubt whether they are strong enough to deter piracy altogether. The solution, say many, is the use of force.

Armed Resistance

In fact, some critics of the nonviolent response to piracy think that lack of arms increases a ship's chance of being pirated. "Merchant ships today are totally at the mercy of anyone who boards them because traditionally merchant ships have never carried arms on board—not even a pistol for self defense,"[43] says Swati Parahar, author of *Maritime Counter-Terrorism: A Pan Asian Perspective*.

This is why some shipowners and even a few government entities, such as the Yemeni Coast Guard, now hire private security firms who provide heavily armed vessels to escort commercial vehicles through pirate-prone seas. Such escorts can cost anywhere from twenty-five thousand to fifty-four thousand dol-

U.S. Marines board the Magellan Star *off the coast of Somalia. The marines captured nine pirates without firing a shot.*

lars for two or three days of protection. Some companies even secure defense training for their own crews.

As the demand for private security rises, so does industry concern over the question of command of the ship. Who, for instance, makes the decision whether to use arms against pirates, the hired security forces or the ship's captain? After private guards aboard the Panama-flagged MV *Almezaan* shot and killed a Somalian pirate in March 2010, other questions emerged. What are the "rules of engagement" when nonmilitary men use lethal force? What kind of training do private guards receive? What kind of people are they? So far there are no industry standards for security guards among shippers. "There's no guarantee of the quality of individuals you are going to get," says piracy expert Roger Middleton from the British think tank Chatham House. "If you're a shipping company, that could be legally concerning. It's also concerning to everyone if you have individuals with guns and not much oversight out on the seas."[44]

Although the shipping industry is divided over the use of private security guards, some within the U.S. military welcome the extra help to properly patrol the Gulf of Aden. The rising use of private security ships to fight piracy in the Gulf of Aden is "a great trend," says Lieutenant Nate Christensen, a spokesman for the Bahrain-based U.S. Fifth Fleet. "We would encourage shipping companies to take proactive measures to help ensure their own safety."[45]

U.S. NAVAL PROTECTION IS KEY TO ENDING PIRACY

"The most desirable and appropriate solution to piracy is for the United States government to provide protection, through military escorts and/or military detachments aboard U.S. vessels."—Richard Phillips, captain of the pirated *Maersk Alabama*

Quoted in *USA Today*. "Former Pirate Hostage: Arming Crews Not the Answer." April 30, 2009. http://content.usatoday.com/communities/ondeadline/post/2009/04/66216053/1.

However, the use of lethal weapons is not a popular choice even among those who support commercial ships defending themselves. For one thing, commercial ships are not built for combat. Nor, for the most part, are merchant crews trained, or willing, to use deadly force. In addition, problems arise when armed guards aboard commercial vessels arrive in ports of foreign lands that ban incoming mariners from bearing arms. When they come into a foreign port, ship captains must declare that there are weapons aboard. At that time customs officials usually confiscate them. Many shipping industry officials also fear that by militarizing their ships they will prompt an "arms race" with the pirates, with each side constantly seeking deadlier and more accurate weaponry.

Shipping companies, as a rule, have been willing to pay ransoms not only to save money, but also to avoid risking the lives of their captains, officers, and crew members. A stray bullet on an oil tanker, for example, could explode the ship, killing all aboard and destroying tens of millions of dollars' worth of cargo and damaging the ship. Conditions, in fact, are so hazardous on oil tankers that there is a ban on smoking and having radios, matches, battery-run devices, and mobile phones on board. As maritime author John Burnett observes, "Jumping off a burning tanker into the flaming sea is a horror never far from those who work these ships. All tankermen live with the fear of a possible collision, a solid bump, anything that can spark ignition."[46]

Exchanging gunfire on the turbulent open seas can also put innocent people in the cross fire between pirates and antipiracy security forces. Sometimes, terrible mistakes can occur. Such was the case in November 2008 when an Indian warship blew a suspected pirate mother ship out of the water, killing fourteen. Later, however, the Indian navy discovered that it had actually

Merchant Marines Speak Out

In March 2010 the Seafarers' International Union, a labor organization that represents merchant marines sailing aboard vessels flagged in the United States, issued a statement on its website clarifying the union's position on how best to combat piracy on the open seas. The following excerpt includes some of those ideas.

> We are proud that throughout our history American merchant mariners have served with distinction as our nation's fourth arm of defense. America's merchant mariners never have and never will shirk their responsibility to deliver the goods whenever and wherever needed.
>
> For this reason, we do not subscribe to an international call for mariners to boycott the waters most at risk to attack by pirates. Rather, we believe that just as land-based criminals know they

> will face strong and swift retribution when they attack innocent victims, we believe seaborne pirates should know they will be treated no differently.
>
> A plan to repel and fight piracy must be as forceful and as unrelenting as piracy itself. We suggested immediately following the attacks against the *Maersk Alabama* and *Liberty Sun* last year that the most effective step that can be taken in response to aggressive action against U.S.-flag ships and their American crews is for our government to provide U.S.-flag vessels with the on-board armed force protection necessary to repel acts of piracy.

Seafarers International Union. "Union Presidents Urge Additional Efforts in Anti-Piracy Campaign." *Seafarers Log*, March 2010. www.seafarers.org/log/2010/032010/piracyletter.xml.

destroyed a Thai trawler that had been hijacked by pirates, and by mistake took the lives of the pirates' victims.

Concern over the use of violence is not the only reason some shipping companies are reluctant to spend money to improve security on their ships. They are also concerned about the cost of security, and most companies prefer governments with trained military forces to handle crimes at sea. "Profit-oriented businesses loathe implementing costly preventive measures, naturally preferring that international organizations, national law enforcement agencies, and armed forces take care of the problem instead," argues retired U.S. Navy commander John Patch. "The international shipping industry thus has a specific interest in exaggerating the global threat of piracy."[47]

International Military Options

Many governments are responding to piracy, even without pressure from the business community. Their main concern is rooted in national self-interest, which, because of the global nature of shipping, is also tied in with the well-being of the international community. In fact, many maritime nations have decided that they have no choice but to band together to fight the growing threat of piracy with force. As authors Jack A. Gottschalk and Brian P. Flanagan write, "Governments, both individually and collectively, represent the only entities with both the motivation and the resources to effectively eradicate or at least decrease maritime piracy."[48]

In 2007 military vessels from Denmark, the Netherlands, and France began escorting World Food Programme (WFP) relief ships to keep pirates from interfering with the delivery of desperately needed humanitarian supplies to 3.2 million impoverished Somalis. Eventually, this program included other European nations and became known as Operation Atlanta. This antipiracy naval operation is still under way off the Somalian coast. In 2008 the United Nations Security Council authorized foreign military vessels to enter and patrol Somalian territorial waters for piracy, provided they obtain permission from the Somalian government.

As part of an international force, an Italian naval vessel escorts a merchant vessel chartered by the World Food Programme as it delivers vital humanitarian aid to Somalia.

Meanwhile, another maritime antipiracy fleet, Operation Ocean Shield, under the control of NATO, is patrolling the region. In addition, the largest antipiracy fleet in history, the Combined Maritime Forces (CMF)—a U.S.-led coalition that includes three dozen ships from Australia, France, Germany, Italy, Pakistan, Canada, Denmark, Turkey, the United States, and the United Kingdom, as well as naval forces from several other nations—now attempts to provide a safe corridor for commercial ships in the Gulf of Aden.

The International Criminal Police Organization (Interpol), operating under the new international legal guidelines, is developing plans to coordinate law enforcement agencies and military units around the world to go after pirates. Similar efforts are under way in Asian nations.

Piracy-weary countries have also banded together to fight piracy in the western Indian Ocean, Gulf of Aden, and Red Sea areas. Some of these nations are taking part in an International Maritime Organization (IMO)–created measure called the Djibouti Code—named for the country where the code was signed on January 26, 2009. Countries that signed the code have pledged to ensure that their national laws make piracy illegal and that their coastal forces have the legal authority to arrest and prosecute pirates in their waters. Moreover, these nations have agreed to cooperate with one another and coordinate their efforts to end piracy. By 2010 Djibouti, Ethiopia, Kenya, Madagascar, Maldives, Seychelles, Somalia, United Republic of Tanzania, and Yemen had signed the agreement.

Help may be forthcoming from the private sector too. According to the International Maritime Bureau (IMB), discussions were under way in the insurance industry in late 2010 as to whether it should raise its own private navy to combat piracy. Supporters believed such a move was needed to augment military antipiracy measures, but critics argued that the presence of a private naval force might persuade governments to reduce the number of military vessels they had already dispatched to piracy hot spots.

Using Military Force

Military forces do more than escort commercial ships through dangerous waters. They also stop and board suspicious-looking boats, confiscate weapons, take pirate suspects into custody and scuttle their boats, so they cannot be used again.

Sometimes military personnel take part in daring chases. Such was the case on April 4, 2008, during a piracy incident that began when eight Somalian pirates traveling in two speed boats, Kalashnikovs blazing, attacked the luxury cruiser *Le Pont* while it was making its way from Seychelles to the Mediterranean. The ship's captain attempted to evade the pirates with a zigzag movement of his vessel, while thirty crew members fixed fire hoses on the pirates. All their efforts proved in vain. The pirates hooked a ladder to the cruiser and swarmed aboard. Then they quickly overpowered the crew members and took them hostage. No passengers, however, were aboard at the time. Soon after the hijacking, French ships and a Canadian helicopter from HMCS *Charlottetown* were shadowing *Le Pont*.

Eight days later, over $2 million in ransom was paid, and the crew was released. But the story was not over. Six French helicopters now swept low over the Somalian coastline and tracked the pirates to a getaway car in a desert. A sniper aboard one of the helicopters fired at the four-wheeled vehicle, hitting the engine block and forcing the vehicle to stop. Six pirates rushed from the disabled car, but they were no match for French commandos who quickly seized them and later sent them to Paris to face piracy charges. The commandos got back about two hundred thousand dollars of the ransom money.

THE SHIPPING INDUSTRY SHOULD FOOT THE BILL

"The international military community cannot be in the business of protecting the financial health of individual businesses. That is the responsibility of the businesses."—Stephen M. Carmel, senior vice president of Maersk Line and merchant ship master

Stephen M. Carmel. "The Big Myth of Somali Pirates." *Proceedings Magazine*, December 2010. www.usni.org/magazines/proceedings/2010-12/big-myth-somali-pirates.

Many maritime security experts wonder whether antipiracy military forces should use even greater force on land targets in Somalia. "Take on the pirates where they are, rather than guessing where they will be. In short, attack them at their home bases,"[49] advises Tom Wilkerson of the U.S. Naval Institute, a nonprofit professional association.

Other analysts, however, think starting a land war in Somalia would only make a bad situation worse. Military attacks against pirate dens, even if authorized by the United Nations, should be "avoided at all costs," because they "will almost certainly have repercussions that go far beyond anything that we have yet witnessed off the Horn [of Africa, where Somalia is]—especially if they result in widespread civilian [deaths,]"[50] warn the authors of a special Rand Corporation report prepared for the U.S. Office of the Secretary of Defense.

Rescue Attempts

Antipiracy military personnel are also called on increasingly to launch daring rescues at sea, which are difficult and dangerous missions to carry out. High drama unfolded in the Indian Ocean in April 2009, for instance, when Somalian pirates boarded and hijacked the U.S.-flagged container ship *Maersk Alabama*, while it attempted to deliver food and supplies to Rwanda, Somalia, and Uganda. The pirates' attempts to commandeer the ship and steer it to Somalia, however, were thwarted when *Maersk Alabama* crew members managed to regain control of the ship. The pirates abandoned the vessel, but not empty-handed. They took the ship's captain, Richard Phillips, with them in a lifeboat. Soon, U.S. warships and a military helicopter appeared on the scene and began shadowing the pirates and their captive. The lifeboat soon ran out of gas. To avoid treacherous high waves that threatened to capsize the boat, the Somalis agreed to be towed by an American warship to safer water. During this maneuver, Phillips dived into the sea to escape, but was forced to return when the pirates fired at him.

A team from the USS Boxer *takes control of the* Maersk Alabama's *lifeboat after navy SEAL snipers shot and killed the three pirates who were holding Captain Richard Phillips onboard.*

Later, it appeared that Phillips's life was in imminent danger when a pirate pointed an AK-47 at his head. Navy officers aboard one of the American ships made a split-second decision and ordered snipers to shoot into the darkness at the pirates. "All of a sudden, shots rang out," Phillips later recalled. "*Bangbangbang-bangbangbang.* . . . As the noise echoed in the tiny boat, I dove into the row of seats, getting as low as I could. I felt something raining down on my face, jabbing my skin. *What now?* I thought. *What just happened?*"[51] Navy SEALs—men of the Sea, Air, Land team who are trained for dangerous missions—soon boarded the boat to rescue him. It was then that Phillips finally looked up from where he crouched in the boat and saw the full extent of what had happened. Three pirates lay dead in the lifeboat. Naval personnel seized a fourth pirate, who was later taken to the United States, where he pleaded guilty to seizing a ship by force and kidnapping. Phillips, along with the crew of the *Maersk Alabama* and the navy commandos, returned to the United States as heroes.

Another daring rescue at sea occurred in May 2010, when Russian commandos stormed the tanker *Moscow University* off the coast of Yemen. A firefight ensued as the Russians battled Somalian hijackers, killing one before disarming and arresting ten other pirates. Next, the Russians freed twenty-three crew members who had turned off the ship's main engine and hidden in a safe room. The pirates were taken back to Russia to stand trial.

Eight months later, in January 2011, South Korean special forces climbed aboard a freighter, the *Samho Jewelry*, which had been hijacked by heavily armed Somalian pirates, in the Arabian Sea. Five hours later, the commandos had rescued twenty-one hostages, killed eight pirates, and taken five others into custody. Though one hostage was wounded, none died during the rescue.

Not all hostages are so lucky. Sometimes they are killed during shootouts between rescuers and their captors. Others are deliberately murdered by pirates. Such was the case when Somalian pirates murdered four Americans in a hijacked yacht off the East African coast in February 2010 just before U.S.

Navy SEALs stormed the craft, subduing and killing some of the pirates.

Whether the use of force deters pirates is yet to be determined. There is evidence that Somalian pirates are merely relocating to avoid military pressure. Some experts suspect that the armed antipiracy fleets will ratchet up the level of violence at sea. Until recently, Somalian pirates had generally refrained from killing their hostages. That policy may be changing. "Every country will be treated the way it treats us," Abdullahi Lami, a self-proclaimed Somalian pirate, told a reporter for the *Independent* following the killing of three pirates by U.S. snipers during the rescue of Captain Phillips in the Gulf of Aden. "In the future, America will be the one mourning and crying. We will retaliate for the killings of our men."[52]

Action in Court

Antipiracy efforts, meanwhile, are under way in courts. By March 2011 seventeen nations had brought more than 850 pirates to trial over the preceding year and a half. The United States is one nation that has taken aggressive steps in court. In November 2010 a federal jury convicted five Somalis on piracy charges for attacking a U.S. Navy ship off Africa's coast. The government announced that the verdict was the first piracy conviction in the United States in nearly two hundred years. The convicted men had fired on the American warship the *Scott* with automatic weapons from their skiff, mistakenly thinking they had come upon a commercial ship they could hold for ransom. Instead, they became the prisoners. "Certainly we hope the word goes forth that armed attacks on U.S.-flagged vessels are crimes against the international community and will not go unpunished,"[53] announced U.S. attorney Neil H. MacBride following the verdict.

Prosecuting pirates, however, is costly. According to One Earth Future's piracy study, "The cost of piracy prosecutions . . . held in three regions: Africa and the Indian Ocean, Europe, and North America . . . [was calculated] in 2010 to be around $31 million."[54]

These prosecutions could intensify a backlash from the pirates. "Somali pirates will now kill hostages," vowed a pirate calling himself Muse Abdi. According to the Associated Press, Abdi vowed revenge for the thirty-three-year prison sentence pirates received for their 2009 attack on the *Maersk Alabama*. "From now on, anyone who tries to rescue the hostages in our hands will only collect dead bodies," the pirate added. "It will never ever happen that hostages are rescued and we are hauled to prison."[55]

Better Reporting

Still more needs to be done to tame the lawless sea, say maritime piracy experts. Some point out that better reporting about piracy attacks is necessary to fully understand how widespread and dangerous piracy has become. A first major step in this direction came in 1992, when the IMB, a division of the International Chamber of Commerce, created the Piracy Reporting Centre (PRC) in Kuala Lumpur, Malaysia. At last, victims of piracy had a place to turn to.

The PRC is not a law enforcement organization, and it does not send help to distressed ships. Instead, it provides a twenty-four-hour reporting service, and it is generally the first place victims report piracy crimes. Many mariners consider the PRC as a sort of 9-1-1 for those who have been terrorized by pirates.

Today the many reports and estimates published by the PRC provide much of the basic information that the seafaring community relies on to keep up with piracy. On its website, the PRC also posts up-to-date alerts of pirate activities around the world and warnings of suspicious commercial transactions that may be linked to goods stolen by pirates.

Gathering this information is not always easy. Some maritime crime investigators believe that crew members of ships that have been victims of piracy are often discouraged, if not punished, by their employers for making known what has happened to them. Shippers, it is suspected, may wish to keep quiet their decisions to pay ransoms. Reporting the crimes, after all, can cause costly delays in shipping schedules.

One solution to this problem may be to set up a system that allows victims of piracy to report attacks anonymously. In addition, argue many industry analysts, the shipping industry itself

Pirates Take the Bridge in Five Minutes

In his book *A Captain's Duty: Somali Pirates Navy SEALs, and Dangerous Days at Sea*, Richard Phillips, captain of the *Maersk Alabama,* describes the takeover of his ship by Somalian pirates, three of whom were later shot dead by U.S. Navy SEALs. The following is an excerpt from *A Captain's Duty*.

I opened my mouth to talk when I thought I saw a shadow in the corner of my eyes. I turned. It was the first pirate, and he was outside the bridge door pointing a battered AK-47 at me through the window.

Just as I turned, the Somali shot off two rounds in the air. POW-WW. POWWW. Up close, that weapon sounded . . . a lot louder than from down below. . . .

"Relax, Captain, relax," the pirate yelled at me. He was short, thin, and wiry. His face was tense. "Business, just business. Stop the ship, stop the ship."

I was so shocked I couldn't answer. I couldn't believe he'd gotten up so fast. He'd gone through the piracy cages like they were child's play.

It was 7.35 a.m. The pirates had taken about five minutes to board my ship and take the bridge.

I still had the portable radio in my hand. I turned my back to the pirate, pressed the key, and, in a low voice, said, "Bridge is compromised, bridge is compromised. Pirates on the bridge." This would let the first engineer in the after steering room know the pirates were in control. "Take the steering," I half-whispered.

"No Al Qaeda, no Al Qaeda, no problem, no problem," the pirate yelled, the AK-47 pointed at my chest. "This is business. We want money only. Stop the ship."

Richard Phillips with Stephen Talty. *A Captain's Duty: Somali Pirates, Navy SEALs, and Dangerous Days at Sea.* New York: Hyperion, 2010, pp. 114–116.

With the lifeboat he was held in behind him, Richard Phillips, captain of the Maersk Alabama, *recounts the harrowing tale of his ship's hijacking and the subsequent high seas rescue by U.S. Navy SEALs.*

must overcome its financial concerns and reveal honestly and openly what it knows about crimes at sea. "And the media have a major responsibility to turn on the switch and shine lights into the dark corners of the world of modern piracy and all of its land-based support systems,"[56] suggest authors Gottschalk and Flanagan. Only with the knowledge gained from full reportage, both by victims and the media, can international law and military force be used appropriately.

Follow the Money

Yet another way to fight piracy is to investigate the economics of piracy. This is especially true as piracy becomes more lucrative and attracts the attention and involvement of crime syndicates. "To strike at the heart of maritime piracy, we must investigate, understand and use to our advantage the financial motivation behind each of these attacks," says Ronald K. Noble, the secretary-general of Interpol, which has the cooperation of 188 countries. "We must follow the money."[57]

In 2009 the London newspaper the *Independent* reported that high-powered businessmen in the Indian subcontinent, the Middle East, and Persian Gulf states are "laundering" vast quantities of money stolen by Somalian pirates. When pirates receive ransom money, they need to quickly exchange it for other currencies to prevent law enforcement officials from tracking down where the money goes. To accomplish this money laundering, bankers are needed. Christopher Ledger, director of Idarat Maritime, a British company specializing in maritime protection, told the newspaper, "There are huge amounts of money involved and this gives the syndicates access to increasingly sophisticated means of moving money as well as access to modern technology in carrying out the hijackings."[58]

A Nation-Building Approach

Many foreign policy analysts agree that military force, deterrence, better reportage, and investigation can all help governments thwart piracy in zones such as the Strait of Malacca that are located near functioning governments. However, they add, something more is needed in areas surrounding failed states such as Somalia. Here, resources and help must also be provided to build up the infrastructure and economic system to improve the conditions that breed piracy in the first place. As former U.S. secretary of defense Robert Gates explains:

> The problem is easier to deal with when the surrounding land—as in the case of Southeast Asia and the Straits of Malacca—is controlled by real governments that have real capabilities, which is not the case in Somalia. So it is a serious international problem, and it's probably going to get worse. There is no purely military solution to it. And as long as you've got this incredible number of poor people and the risks are relatively small, there's really no way in my view to control it unless you get something on land that begins to change the equation for these kids [i.e., the pirates, who are generally young].[59]

But questions remain, such as: What kind of help would be offered? Who would receive it? The Somalian government? Clan leaders? Who pays for this economic assistance? What if Somalis do not want change?

Creating Worse Pirates?

As nations struggle to answer such questions, many analysts also fear that the current antipiracy efforts could backfire and end up encouraging a "survival of the fittest" process that may produce an even more ruthless and efficient form of piracy to emerge. They argue that the world's powerful navies may be able only to destroy or capture the world's weakest pirates. If so, the more cunning and ruthless ones will be left to dominate the world of piracy. As Michael G. Frodl, an emerging risks adviser warns, "Fourth generation piracy is sure to appear sooner than later if we keep leaving the initiative to the best Somali gangs. Current counter-piracy approaches make it ironically even easier for them to reap most of the rewards, as their less capable competitors are eliminated, leaving the ocean and its richest prizes for them."[60] If so, nations may be even more at risk on the open seas. And that is not their only problem.

PREPARING FOR
THE WORST

Piracy is not the only growing danger that seafarers must face. Terrorism at sea is another. Around the world come reports of terrorist groups that commit mass murder and torture and inflict terror on entire societies for religious or political purposes. As these terrorists seek new ways to wreak havoc, many security experts fear it is just a matter of time until the worlds of piracy and terrorism merge or overlap.

But what is terrorism? "While there are internationally agreed upon legal definitions of what constitutes piracy and maritime crime, there are no similar statutes defining terrorism. This may be because one person's terrorist is another's freedom fighter,"[61] argues author Daniel Sekulich.

Although both pirates and terrorists are violent, malicious, and generally not associated with any particular government, there are stark differences between the two groups. Pirates, for instance, are, above all else, criminals who seek opportunities to commit crimes to get money quickly. Few if any risk their lives for political reasons alone.

Terrorists on the other hand almost always have political goals. In fact, many consider themselves "freedom fighters," or insurgents, that are courageously combating evil opponents. Some use terror as a means of driving foreign troops from their countries. Others seek to topple a hated government or to crush rival religious, ethnic, or racial groups. Sometimes, terror is also used to inflict punishment or revenge, which may be the motive of the Islamist terrorist group al Qaeda, which attacked the United States on September 11, 2001.

Piracy May Serve as a "Platform" for Terrorist Attacks

In a *New York Times* op-ed article, Robert Kaplan, a national correspondent for the *Atlantic Monthly* and a senior fellow at the Center for a New American Security, explains why he thinks piracy will attract terrorists:

> The big danger in our day is that piracy can potentially serve as a platform for terrorists. Using pirate techniques, vessels can be hijacked and blown up in the middle of a crowded strait, or a cruise ship seized and the passengers of certain nationalities thrown overboard. You can see how Al Qaeda would be studying this latest episode at sea, in which Somali pirates attacked a Maersk Line container ship and were fought off by the American crew, even as they have managed to take the captain hostage in one of the lifeboats.

Robert D. Kaplan. "Anarchy on Land Means Piracy at Sea." *New York Times*, April 11, 2009. www.nytimes.com/2009/04/12/opinion/12kaplan.html.

Terrorism experts say the big danger today is that piracy can potentially serve as a platform for terrorists using piracy techniques.

According to many security specialists, terrorists constantly seek new ways to strike at their enemies. Some consider the world of maritime commerce as rich with opportunities for spreading their terror. A common fear expressed in the maritime security community is that terrorists may one day blow up a cruise ship or a slow-moving tanker filled with oil, liquid nitrogen, or ammonium nitrate—a key ingredient in many fertilizers—in one of the world's narrow "chokepoints," such as the Malacca Strait or Egypt's Suez Canal. Such a blasted vessel could clog sea traffic, disrupt energy supplies to Western nations like the United States, and cause a massive environmental catastrophe.

Overlapping Worlds

Though pirates and terrorists inhabit different worlds, there is evidence that their two realms may be merging. As governments crack down on terrorist organizations and interrupt or freeze their bank accounts, some terrorists have hired pirates to carry out attacks at sea on their behalf. Such may be the case in Somalia. Al-Shabaab—a militant Islamist group that emerged in Somalia after the fall of the Islamic Courts—is suspected by the CIA and other intelligence-gathering groups of hiring Somalian pirate gangs to smuggle arms into Somalia.

Other terrorists, however, do not need the help of pirates. Instead, they appear to have taken up the techniques of maritime piracy themselves, to expand their attacks of terrorism to ships at sea.

Suicide Attacks in Yemen

On January 3, 2000, al Qaeda launched its first pirate-like attack on an American warship, *The Sullivans*, while it was tied up at Aden, a port city in the Republic of Yemen, a country located on the Arabian Peninsula. The attempt failed, however, when the boat, carrying suicide bombers, sank because it was overloaded with explosives.

Al Qaeda struck again on October 12. This time the attack was against the USS *Cole*, a billion-dollar guided-missile destroyer, also moored at Aden. At about 11:18 A.M., local time, a speedboat appeared in the harbor carrying a pair of suicide

The USS Cole shows a gaping hole in her side. The damage was caused by a terrorist suicide bomber who rammed the ship with a boat loaded with an estimated 1,000 pounds of explosives.

bombers and an estimated 1,000 pounds (453.5kg) of explosives. The 15-foot skiff (4.5m) circled the American ship and then suddenly rammed into its port side, setting off an explosion which blew a 40- to 60-foot hole (12m to 18m) in the warship. The explosion killed the bombers and seventeen sailors, and it injured thirty-nine other members of the crew.

U.S. investigators concluded that the suicide attack was planned by a man known as Abd al-Rahim al-Nashiri, a citizen of Saudi Arabia and an associate of Osama bin Laden, the leader of al Qaeda. Following the attack al-Nashiri obtained a nickname from fellow terrorists: the Prince of the Sea.

Two years later, in the fall of 2002, al-Nashiri's men allegedly targeted a large French-flagged vessel, the MV *Limburg*. As the supertanker approached the Ash Shihr oil terminal not far from the port of Mukalla, Yemen, two suicide killers crashed their fiberglass boat into the ship, blowing themselves up, killing one crew member, and injuring twenty-five others. The explosion blasted through the double-hulled tanker, leaving a 36-by-26-foot gash (10.9m by 7.9m), and rupturing containers on board the *Limburg*, which spilled anywhere from fifty thousand to ninety thousand barrels of crude oil into the Gulf of Aden.

Two months following this attack, Yemeni authorities arrested al-Nashiri. They turned him over to American officials, who placed him in a detention center for suspected terrorists at the American naval base in Guantánamo Bay, Cuba.

Boat Attacks by Tamil Tigers

Meanwhile in South Asia, the Tamil Tigers—a militant group of Hindus—were also using boats filled with explosives for suicide attacks against Sri Lankan military vessels, as a part of their ongoing effort to gain independence from Buddhist-dominated Sri Lanka, a country located off the southeastern coast of the Indian subcontinent.

THE NEED FOR NEW LAWS

"We're dealing with a very new form of piracy and the big question for the politicians is whether that should justify a different application of a legal system than the ordinary law enforcement system."—Dutch international criminal lawyer Geert-Jan Knoops

Quoted in Hermione Gee. "Modern Piracy Needs Modern Laws, says Dutch Lawyer." Radio Netherlands, April 16, 2009. http://static.rnw.nl/migratie/www.rnw.nl/inter nationaljustice/specials/Universal/090416-modern-piracy-laws-redirected.

Deadly attacks also took place against innocent foreigners who had nothing to do with the conflict in Sri Lanka. On March 20, 2003, for example, several fast-moving small boats off the coast of Sri Lanka, circled an unarmed Chinese fishing trawler, the *Yuan Yu 225*. Suddenly, gunmen opened fire with automatic weapons, raking the fishing boat with bullets until it sank. The attackers kept firing upon the Chinese men, even as they struggled in the water, wearing life preservers. By the time the shooting stopped, seventeen were dead. Nine victims who survived the ordeal later blamed the atrocity on the Tamil Tigers, who, however, denied responsibility. The Sri Lankan navy also denied having a role in the attack. The real culprits may never be known for sure.

Death in the Philippines

Terror at sea has also come to the Philippines, a country composed of over seven thousand islands located in Southeast Asia in the western Pacific Ocean. In February 2004 in the country's capital city of Manila, almost nine hundred passengers boarded *SuperFerry 14* to make a routine overnight trip to the islands of Bacolod and Davao. Among those who came aboard was a young man calling himself Arnulfo Alvarado, but whose real name was Redondo Cain Dellosa.

Ferry authorities failed to recognize that Dellosa was a member of Abu Sayyaf, a violent Muslim group with al Qaeda ties. Abbu Sayyaf has long waged a brutal struggle against the Philippine government to establish a separate, Islam-based government in the southern Philippines. The authorities also failed to notice that buried deep in the television which Alvardo took aboard the ferry in a cardboard box that night were explosives and a timer.

Dellosa left his deadly cargo in a crowded area below the main deck and slipped off the ferry before it departed at 11 P.M.

The Philippine SuperFerry 14 *lies on its side after an attack by Redondo Cain Dellosa of the Abu Sayyaf terrorist group. The attack killed over one hundred people.*

An hour later the bomb exploded, killing passengers and destroying a large area of the ferry. A deadly fire suddenly whipped across the distressed ship, causing hundreds of terror-stricken passengers to leap into the night sea. Altogether, over one hundred people died as a result of the attack and the ensuing mayhem, making it the deadliest terrorist attack in Philippine history and the world's deadliest attack at sea.

Terrorist Hijackings at Sea

Terrorists have been hijacking ships for decades. Unlike many pirates, whose motives usually involve robbery and extortion, terrorists have seized vessels at sea to maim, terrorize, kill, and create sensational headlines around the world to promote their political crusades. One such group is the Palestine Liberation Organization (PLO)—a political and military organization that once professed a goal to destroy Israel and create an independent state for Palestinians. The United States has long considered the PLO a terrorist organization because of attacks carried out by its members.

One such attack occurred on October 7, 1985, when four PLO terrorists hijacked the Italian luxury cruise liner *Achille Lauro* on its way from Egypt to Israel. During the seizure the terrorists murdered Leon Klinghoffer, an elderly wheelchair-bound Jewish American citizen, and threw his body into the sea.

Palestinian terrorists made another maritime strike on the evening of July 11, 1988, when they stormed the *City of Poros*, a Greek passenger ferry with 471 persons on board, as it traveled to the island Aegina. Using automatic weapons and grenades, they attacked passengers, some of whom jumped overboard and were killed by the ship's propellers. The final casualties included 11 dead and 98 injured. A distress call went out, and soon ships in the area came to help, but by then the killers had escaped. Most likely, say investigators, the motive for this sea crime was to retaliate against legal efforts to extradite a Palestinian in Greek custody to the United States to stand trial for terrorism.

International Response

Such crimes as these have convinced many maritime experts that piracy and terrorism, despite their differences, are two sides of the same coin, especially in the Gulf of Aden. "When addressing the alarming rise in piracy off Somalia, we must not overlook the emerging alliance between piracy and terrorism," writes Lieutenant Commander Akash Chaturvedi, of the Indian navy. "To win the battles against . . . [them], they need to be perceived as one battle."[62]

To view piracy and terrorism as the same battle, nations may need to reconsider how they define pirates and terrorists. Both, suggest author Douglas R. Burgess, are enemies of mankind and should be treated by international law in the same way. "Are pirates a species of terrorist?" he asks in an opinion editorial for the *New York Times*. "In short, yes."[63] And what's more, he adds, "It seems sensible that the United States and the international community adopt a new, shared legal definition that would recognize the link between piracy and terrorism. This could take

Terrorism and Piracy Combine in Asia

Chinese maritime researcher Hong Nong contends in *Maritime Security in the South China Sea* that terrorism and piracy are on the rise in Asia and are connected. The following is an excerpt from that book.

The interweaving of maritime piracy and terrorism has tended to threaten regional security in Asia. Piracy in the high sea has gradually been used as the tool for terrorist groups. The interrelation between piracy and terrorism poses great threat to the energy market since oil and natural gas transportation are mostly through the areas where piracy happened most frequently. Pirates and Islamic terrorists have been acting jointly in the Arabian Sea, the South China Sea, and the West Africa coastal area. Since the international community has worked hard to freeze the capital [funds] of terrorist groups, they tend to acquire funds through the activities of pirates. Maritime attacks in recent years have shown that terrorism has expanded to the sea.

Hong Nong. "Maritime Trade Development in Asia: A Need for Regional Maritime Security Cooperation in the South China Sea." *Maritime Security in the South China Sea*. Schicun Wu and Keyuan Zou, eds. Surrey, England: Ashgate, 2009, p 41.

the form of an act of Congress or, more broadly, a new jurisdiction for piracy and terrorism cases at the International Criminal Court."[64] Such a system, Burgess argues, would allow nations to hunt down and arrest both pirates and terrorists anywhere in the world, and the international court would be available for those that do not want to prosecute.

Sorting Out the Responsibility

"The distinction between piracy and terrorism is neither semantic nor academic. If piracy, the responsibility lies with local law enforcement officials, not the military. But maritime terrorism means scrambling the Navy."—retired U.S. Navy commander John Patch

John Patch. "The Overstated Threat." *Proceedings Magazine*, December 2008. www.usni. org/magazines/proceedings/2008-12/overstated-threat.

Some analysts believe that the lessons learned from fighting pirates can assist nations in combating terrorism at sea. International cooperation among the world's navies, judicial systems, intelligence-gathering organizations, law enforcement agencies, and political systems are what is needed to bring order to the lawless seas, whether those disruptions are caused by piracy or terrorism. Such a unified worldwide strategy to address the lawless seas may be long overdue. A never-ending dark and disturbing parade of problems, such as financial meltdowns, wars, political and religious unrest, famine, poverty, and a host of other social ills will continue to contribute to piracy—and possibly maritime terrorism—unless the world community commits its resources to attacking the rising threats to seafarers.

At the same time, the mariners themselves will do what they can to help. As Shane Murphy, chief mate on the *Maersk Alabama*, freed from Somalian pirates by U.S. Navy commandos, told television journalist Ray Suarez, "At sea, it's a global community. It doesn't come down to nations. There's a whole world out there at sea that we live [in] together. We look out for each other."[65]

Introduction: Anarchy at Sea

1. One Earth Future, Oceans Beyond Piracy. "The Economic Costs of Maritime Piracy." http://oceansbeyondpiracy.org/documents/The_Economic_Cost_of_Piracy_Full_Report.pdf.

Chapter 1: The Rise of Modern Pirates

2. International Marine Bureau Piracy Reporting Centre. "Hostage-Taking at Sea Rises to Record Levels, Says IMB." www.icc-ccs.org/news/429-hostage-taking-at-sea-rises-to-record-levels-says-imb.

3. Quoted in International Marine Bureau Piracy Reporting Centre, "Hostage-Taking at Sea Rises."

4. John S. Burnett. Prologue to *Dangerous Waters: Modern Piracy and Terror on the High Seas.* New York: Dutton, Penguin, 2002, p. 10.

5. Daniel Sekulich. *Terror on the Seas: True Tales of Modern-Day Pirates.* New York: St. Martin's, 2009, p. 104.

6. Quoted in Sekulich, *Terror on the Seas: True Tales of Modern-Day Pirates,* p. 192.

7. Quoted in Noah Shachtman. "Exclusive Interview: Pirate on When to Negotiate, Kill Hostages." *Wired,* July 28, 2009. www.wired.com/dangerroom/2009/07/exclusive-interview-pirate-on-when-to-negotiate-kill-hostages/.

8. Volker Bertram. "Technologies for Low Crew/No Crew Ships." http://utopia.duth.gr/~agaster/papers/cite/Ships.pdf.

9. Peter Chalk. "Maritime Piracy, Dangers, Solutions." The Rand Corporation. Testimony presented before the House Transportation and Infrastructure Subcommittee on Coast Guard and Maritime Transportation, February 2009. www.rand.org/pubs/testimonies/2009/RAND_CT317.pdf .

10. Chalk, "Maritime Piracy, Dangers, Solutions."

11. John S. Burnett. "Captain Kidd, Human-Rights Victim." *New York Times*, April 20, 2008. www.nytimes.com/2008/04/20/opinion/20burnett.html.

12. International Whaling Commission. "Statement of Safety at Sea." http://iwcoffice.org/meetings/intersession08.htm#safety.

13. Sea Shepherd. "Sea Shepherd Responds to Japanese Whaling Industry Propaganda." January 3, 2009. http://de.seashepherd.org/news-and-media/news-090103-1.html.

Chapter 2: The Most Pirate-Infested Waters in the World

14. Quoted in Shachtman, "Exclusive Interview."

15. Quoted in Jason Straziuso. "Kenya Fishermen See Upside to Pirates: More Fish." Associated Press/Hiiraan Online. www.hiiraan.com/news2/2010/jan/kenya_fishermen_see_upside_to_pirates_more_fish.aspx.

16. Quoted in Robyn Hunter. "Somali Pirates Living the High Life." BBC News, October 8, 2009. http://news.bbc.co.uk/2/hi/africa/7650415.stm.

17. Quoted in Shashank Bengali. "An Interview with a Jailed Somali Pirate Leader." *Christian Science Monitor*, May 3, 2009. www.csmonitor.com/World/Africa/2009/0503/p06s12-woaf.html.

18. Quoted in Scott Baldauf. "Who Are Somalia's Pirates?" *Christian Science Monitor*, November 20, 2008. www.csmonitor.com/World/Africa/2008/1120/p25s22-woaf.html.

19. Quoted in Sekulich, *Terror on the Seas,* pp. 164–165.

20. Quoted in Sekulich, *Terror on the Seas,* pp. 164–165.

21. Quoted in Interview by Xan Rice and Abdiqani Hassan. "'We Consider Ourselves Heroes'—a Somali Pirate Speaks." *Guardian* (Manchester, UK), November 22, 2008. www.guardian.co.uk/world/2008/nov/22/piracy-somalia.

Chapter 3: Piracy Hot Spots Around the World

22. Alex Perry. "Buccaneer Tales in the Pirates' Lair." *Time* Asia, August 20–27, 2001. www.time.com/time/asia/features/journey2001/pirates.html.

23. Burnett, *Dangerous Waters*, p. 234.

24. Quoted in Charles Glass. "The New Piracy." *London Review of Books*, December 18, 2003. www.lrb.co.uk/v25/n24/charles-glass/the-new-piracy.

25. Bertil Lintner. *Blood Brothers: The Criminal Underworld of Asia*. New York: Palgrave MacMillan, 2003. Extract, Asia Pacific Media Services Ltd. www.asiapacificms.com/books/blood_brothers.php.

26. Lintner, *Blood Brothers*.

27. Vivay Sakhuja. "Sea Piracy in South Asia." In *Violence at Sea: Piracy in the Age of Global Terrorism,* edited by Peter Lehr. New York, London: Taylor & Francis, 2007, pp. 26.

28. Guy Matthews. "Modern Pirates of the Caribbean." BluewaterInsurance.com. www.bluewaterins.com/second/pirates.htm.

Chapter 4: Piracy and the Law

29. Sekulich, *Terror on the Seas,* p. 86.

30. United Nations. *Convention on the High Seas.* United Nations Treaty Series, vol. 450, 1958, pp. 11, 82. http://untreaty.un.org/ILC/TEXTS/INSTRUMENTS/ENGLISH/CONVENTIONS/8_1_1958_HIGH_SEAS.PDF.

31. United Nations. United Nations Convention on the Law of the Sea. December 10, 1982. www.un.org/Depts/los/convention_agreements/texts/unclos/unclos_e.pdf.

32. Hermione Gee. "Modern Piracy Needs Modern Laws, Says Dutch Lawyer." Radio Netherlands, April 16, 2009. http://static.rnw.nl/migratie/www.rnw.nl/internationaljustice/specials/Universal/090416-modern-piracy-laws-redirected.

33. Burnett, *Dangerous Waters*, p. 160.

34. Quoted in Neal Hodge. "Trouble at Sea." International Bar Association. www.ibanet.org/Article/Detail.aspx?ArticleUid=09cadd50-52f7-49d6-ae4d-6b95aaacad25.

Chapter 5: The Damaging Impact of Piracy

35. One Earth Future, Oceans Beyond Piracy, "The Economic Costs of Piracy."

36. Quoted in Jason Straziuso. "Are Ransoms Legal? Confusion over US Order." Associated Press/Hiiraan Online. www.hi

iraan.com/news2/2010/apr/are_pirate_ransoms_legal_con
fusion_over_us_order.aspx.

37. Burnett, *Dangerous Waters,* p. 213.

38. Jim Walker. "Cruise Line Liability for Injuries to Passengers and Crew Members Caused by Pirate Attacks." Cruise Law News, November 19, 2009. www.cruiselawnews .com/2009/11/articles/pirate-attacks/cruise-line-liability-for-injuries-to-passengers-and-crew-members-caused-by-pirate-attacks/.

39. John C. Payne. *Piracy Today.* Dobbs Ferry, NY: Sheridan House, 2010, p. 33.

40. Quoted in Daniel Howden. "I Don't Even Tell My Company What Route I'm Taking." *Independent* (London), April 21, 2009. www.independent.co.uk/news/world/africa/ piracy-i-dont-even-tell-my-company-what-route-im-taking-1671659.html.

Chapter 6: Fighting Back

41. Quoted in BBC News. "Somali Vigilantes Capture Pirates." April 28, 2009. http://news.bbc.co.uk/2/hi/africa/8022820 .stm.

42. Quoted in Allianz Global Corporate & Specialty. "Piracy, an Ancient Risk with Modern Face," June 22, 2009, p. 16. www.agcs.allianz.com/assets/PDFs/risk%20insights/Alli anz%20Piracy%20Study%20-%20June%202009.pdf.

43. Swati Parashar. *Maritime Counter-Terrorism: A Pan Asian Perspective.* New Delhi: Pearson Education, 2008, p. 9.

44. Quoted in Katherine Houreld. "Private Guards Kill Somali Pirate for First Time." ABC News, March 24, 2010. http:// abcnews.go.com/International/wireStory?id=10186774.

45. Quoted in Katharine Houreld. "Private Security Firms Join Fights Against Pirates." *Columbus (OH) Dispatch,* October 27, 2008. www.dispatch.com/live/content/ national_world/stories/2008/10/27/somali_piracy_1027 .ART_ART_10-27-08_A6_JKBNBJB.html.

46. Burnett, *Dangerous Waters,* p. 149.

47. John Patch. "The Overstated Threat." *Proceedings Magazine,* December 2008. www.usni.org/magazines/proceed ings/2008-12/overstated-threat.

48. Jack A. Gottschalk and Brian P. Flanagan, with Lawrence J. Kahn and Dennis M. LaRochelle. *Jolly Rogers with an Uzi: The Rise and Threat of Modern Piracy*. Annapolis, MD: Naval Institute Press, 2000, pp. 107–108.

49. Quoted in Arthur Bright. "Critics Say U.S. Should Attack Somali Pirates' Land Bases." *Christian Science Monitor*, April 10, 2009. www.csmonitor.com/Commentary/Letters-to-the-Editor/2009/0410/p99s01-cole.html.

50. Peter Chalk, Laurence Smallman, and Nicholas Burger. "Countering Piracy in the Modern Era," Notes from a Rand National Defense Research Institute Workshop to Discuss the Best Approaches for Dealing with Piracy in the 21st Century, 2009. www.rand.org/pubs/conf_proceedings/2009/RAND_CF269.pdf.

51. Richard Phillips with Stephan Talty. *A Captain's Duty: Somali Pirates, Navy SEALs, and Dangerous Days at Sea*. New York: Hyperion, 2010, p. 261.

52. Quoted in Daniel Howden. "Pirates Promise to Take Their Revenge Against US." *Independent* (London), April 14, 2009. www.independent.co.uk/news/world/Africa/pirates-promise- to-take-their-revenge-against-us-1668266.html.

53. Quoted in Steve Szkotak. "US Jury Convicts Somalis as Pirates in Navy Attack." Newsvine.com, November 23, 2010. www.newsvine.com/_news/2010/11/23/5514644-us-jury-convicts-somalis-as-pirates-in-navy-attack.

54. One Earth Future, Oceans Beyond Piracy, "The Economic Costs of Piracy." http://oceansbeyondpiracy.org/documents/The_Economic_Cost_of_Piracy_Full_Report.pdf.

55. Quoted in CBS News. "4 Americans on Hijacked Yacht Dead off Somalia," February 22, 2011. www.cbsnews.com/stories/2011/02/22/501364/main20034691.shtml.

56. Gottschalk, Flanagan, Kahn, and LaRochelle, *Jolly Rogers with an Uzi*, p. 143.

57. Ronald K. Noble. "Conference on Maritime Piracy Financial Investigations." Welcome Address, January 19–20, 2010. www.interpol.int/Public/ICPO/speeches/2010/SGMaritimePiracy20100119.asp.

58. Quoted in Sengupta and Daniel Howden. "Pirates: The $80m Gulf Connection." *Independent* (London), April 21, 2009. www.independent.co.uk/news/world/africa/pirates-the-80m-gulf-connection-1671657.html.

59. Quoted in John J. Kreuzel. "Secretary Robert M. Gates Says Navy's Rescue Mission 'Textbook,' but Piracy Still Looms." United States Department of Defense. www.militaryrates.com/military-news-story.cfm?textnewsid=2987.

60. Michael G. Frodl. "Somali Piracy Tactics Evolve; Threats Could Expand Globally." *National Defense Magazine,* April 2010. www.nationaldefensemagazine.org/archive/2010/April/Pages/SomaliPiracyTacticsEvolve.aspx.

Chapter 7: Preparing for the Worst

61. Sekulich, *Terror on the Seas,* p. 223.

62. Quoted in Akash Chaturvedi. "Two Faces of High-Seas Crime." *Proceedings Magazine*, July 2010. www.usni.org/magazines/proceedings/2010-07/two-faces-high-seas-crime.

63. Douglas, R. Burgess. "Piracy Is Terrorism." *New York Times*, December 5, 2008. www.nytimes.com/2008/12/05/opinion/05burgess.html.

64. Burgess, "Piracy Is Terrorism."

65. PBS Newshour. "Combating Piracy Poses New Challenge for U.S. Ships." www.pbs.org/newshour/bb/africa/jan-june09/pirates_04-13.html.

DISCUSSION QUESTIONS

Chapter 1: The Rise of Modern Pirates

1. Why has modern piracy become a "hot issue" in recent years?
2. What are the three basic levels of modern piracy?
3. Explain how modern pirates are making use of new technology and communications devices.

Chapter 2: The Most Pirate-Infested Waters in the World

1. Describe how the breakdown in law and order in Somalia led to the rise of piracy in that country.
2. Why are some Somalian pirates admired by many other Somalis?
3. Why are some Islamic militants opposed to piracy in Somalia?

Chapter 3: Piracy Hot Spots Around the World

1. Why have some Nigerians, such as those in MEND, turned to piracy in recent years?
2. Describe how the governments of Indonesia, Singapore, and Malaysia have slowed down piracy in recent years.
3. What are some other piracy hot spots in the world?

Chapter 4: Piracy and the Law

1. Why do some nations differ over what piracy is?
2. What are some problems faced by countries that try to enforce piracy laws on the open seas?
3. Describe some of the human rights concerns that legal experts have raised over the prosecution of piracy suspects.

Chapter 5: The Damaging Impact of Piracy

1. Summarize the various kinds of economic costs that piracy inflicts on others.
2. Describe several legal problems caused by piracy that are faced by the shipping industry.
3. What are some of the noneconomic costs caused by piracy?

Chapter 6: Fighting Back

1. Describe several ways, other than the use of force, that shipping companies are deterring pirates.
2. Summarize the arguments for and against using armed resistance against piracy.
3. Name some of the nations that have sent their navies to piracy hot spots.

Chapter 7: Preparing for the Worst

1. How do piracy and terrorism differ? How are they similar?
2. Describe how the worlds of piracy and terrorism may overlap.
3. Explain why piracy experts say a unified, international response is needed to end piracy.

Combined Task Force 151 (CTF 151)
Public Affairs Officer
PSC 901 Box 12
FPO AE 09805-0001
Phone: 011-973-1785-4027.
E-mail: navcentpao@me.navy.mil
Website: www.cusnc.navy.mil/cmf/cmf.html

CTF 151 is a multinational task force whose naval vessels function as part of the Combined Maritime Forces (CMF) to deter and stop piracy in the Gulf of Aden and to provide security for ships traveling through the region.

European Union (EU)
Europe House
32 Smith Sq.
London, England SW1P 3EU
Phone: +44 (0)20 7227 4300
Website: http://europa.eu/about-eu?index_en.htm

The EU is an economic and political organization of twenty-seven European member states. Its members retain the right to self-govern but also combine their resources to gain power and influence at the international level. Naval forces from many of the EU's members provide protection from piracy for humanitarian convoys and fishing fleets off the Somalian coast.

Institute for the Analysis of Global Security (IAGS)
7811 Montrose Rd., Ste. 505
Potomac, MD 20854
Phone: (866) 713-7527
E-mail: info@iags.org
Website: www.iags.org

The IAGS is a nonprofit organization specializing in matters concerning America's oil security, including those posed by maritime piracy.

International Maritime Bureau (IMB)
Cinnabar Wharf 26 Wapping High St.
London, England E1W 1NG
Phone: +44 (0)20 7423 6960
Fax: +44 (0)20 7423 6961
Website: www.icc-ccs.org/home/imb

The IMB is a division of the International Chamber of Commerce (ICC), a nonprofit organization established to fight maritime crime. It also manages the ICC Commercial Crime Services which has links to the IMB Piracy Reporting Centre (PRC), an organization that is the leading provider of piracy reports for the world.

International Maritime Organization (IMO)
4 Albert Embankment
London
SE1 7SR
United Kingdom
Phone: +44 (0)20 7735 7611
Fax: +44 (0)20 7587 3210
E-mail: info@imo.org
Website: www.imo.org/Pages/home.aspx

The IMO is the United Nations specialized agency charged with ensuring the safety and security of shipping and the preventing marine pollution caused by ships. It has also recognized piracy as a maritime danger.

Interpol
General Secretariat
200, quai Charles de Gaulle
69006 Lyon, France
Fax: +33 (0)4 72 44 71 63
Website: www.interpol.int/Public/contact.asp

Interpol is the world's largest international police organization. Among its many tasks is prosecuting cases of maritime piracy.

North Atlantic Treaty Organization (NATO)

Website: www.nato.int/cps/en/natolive/index.htm

Headquartered in Brussels, Belgium, this major military alliance of democratic states in Europe and North America provides collective military security to its member states in North America and Western Europe. As part of its antipiracy activities, the organization provides military escorts to UN World Food Programme vessels traveling through pirate-infested waters in the Gulf of Aden. NATO vessels also provide surveillance and deterrence patrols. Its website offers articles describing its antipiracy programs.

One Earth Future (OEF)

1450 Infinite Dr., E-1
Louisville, CO 80027
Phone: (303) 533-1715
E-mail: officedirector@oneearthfuture.org; info@oneearth future.org
Website: http://oneearthfuture.org/index.php?id=11&page= Contact_Us

OEF is a Colorado-based nonprofit think tank established to develop effective systems of solving global problems without war. Among the organization's research projects is its flagship *Ocean Beyond Privacy* report that focuses on causes and impacts of maritime piracy, along with peaceful solutions to the ongoing problem.

Seafarers International Union (SIU)

5201 Auth Way, Camp Springs, MD 20746
Phone: (301) 899-0675
Fax: (301) 899-7355
Website: www.seafarers.org

The SIU represents the merchant marines that sail aboard U.S. flagships in the deep sea, Great Lakes, and inland waterways. Its members recently launched a "Save Our Seafarers" campaign to put pressure on nations around the world to take action against maritime piracy.

Books

Noah Berlatsky, ed. *Piracy on the High Seas*. Detroit: Greenhaven Press, 2010. This edition of the At Issue series contains a wide range of expert opinions on modern piracy, including primary and secondary sources.

Internet Sources

Carole D. Bos. "Pirates of the Caribbean." Awesome Stories. com. www.awesomestories.com/flicks/pirates-caribbean>. An educational website with numerous informative stories about seventeenth-century piracy.

New York Times. "Piracy at Sea." A webpage with links to hundreds of *New York Times* articles about modern piracy. http://topics.nytimes.com/top/reference/timestopics/subjects/p/piracy_at_sea/index.html.

Cindy Vallar, ed. Pirates and Privateers: The History of Maritime Piracy. www.cindyvallar.com/pirates.html. This website contains scores of articles covering a wide range of topics related to maritime piracy from ancient times to modern day, along with links to other useful sites.

Websites

Admiralty and Maritime Law Guide (www.admiraltylawguide. com/index.html). Authored by Todd Kenyon, a member of a New Jersey–based law firm specializing in maritime law. This site, recommended by many colleges of law, offers over fifteen hundred annotated links to admiralty law resources, along with a database of summaries of admiralty, legal opinions, and international maritime agreements.

Cargo Security International (www.cargosecurityinternation al.com). A British subscription online service with piracy updates for the transport industry.

Federation of American Scientists (www.fas.org/main/search. jsp). An independent, nonpartisan think tank for the scientific community that offers piracy updates on modern piracy.

Field Museum (http://archive.fieldmuseum.org/pirates/high lights.asp). "Real Pirates." Exhibition Highlights, Chicago's Field Museum website that complemented a public pirate exhibit, with many links and tabs related to articles about piracy past and present.

International Maritime Bureau (www.iccwbo.org). The IMB established the twenty-four-hour IMB Piracy Reporting Centre (PRC) in Kuala Lumpur, Malaysia, a nongovernmental organization that tracks and reports pirate activity around the world.

International Maritime Organization (IMO) (www.imo.org/ home.asp). Headquartered in London, England, the IMO is a specialized agency of the United Nations whose website offers information on piracy and other shipping matters.

Interpol (www.interpol.com/Public/Terrorism/). Interpol, the world's largest international police organization, provides news on maritime piracy at is website.

Maritime Security (www.maritimesecurity.com/contact.htm). Sponsored by Favor Bold Marine, a Ft. Lauderdale, Florida– based firm, features at its website recent news and commentary on modern piracy.

Noonsite (www.noonsite.com/General/Piracy). A private website offering current and past reports of piracy and other information for seafarers planning a voyage anywhere in the world.

Oceans and Law of the Sea (www.un.org/Depts/los/conven tion_agreements/texts/unclos/UNCLOS-TOC.htm). This website contains the United Nations Convention on the Law of the Sea of 10 December 1982, a document of international agreements pertaining to piracy

ONI WorldWide Threat to Shipping (http://msi.nga.mil/ NGAPortal/MSI.portal). This website is part of the National Geospatial-Intelligence Agency, a federal government entity that provides reports by date of maritime warnings, including piracy.

INDEX

PICTURE CREDITS

119

ABOUT THE AUTHOR

John M. Dunn is a writer and veteran high school social studies teacher. He has published numerous articles in more than twenty periodicals, as well as scripts for audio-visual productions and a children's play. Other Lucent Books titles by Dunn include *The Russian Revolution, The Relocation of the North American Indian, The Spread of Islam, Advertising, The Civil Rights Movement, The Enlightenment, Life During the Black Death, The Vietnam War: A History of U.S. Involvement, The Computer Revolution, The French Revolution: The Fall of the Monarchy, Life in Castro's Cuba, The Constitution and Founding of America,* and *Prohibition.* Dunn lives with his wife in Ocala, Florida.